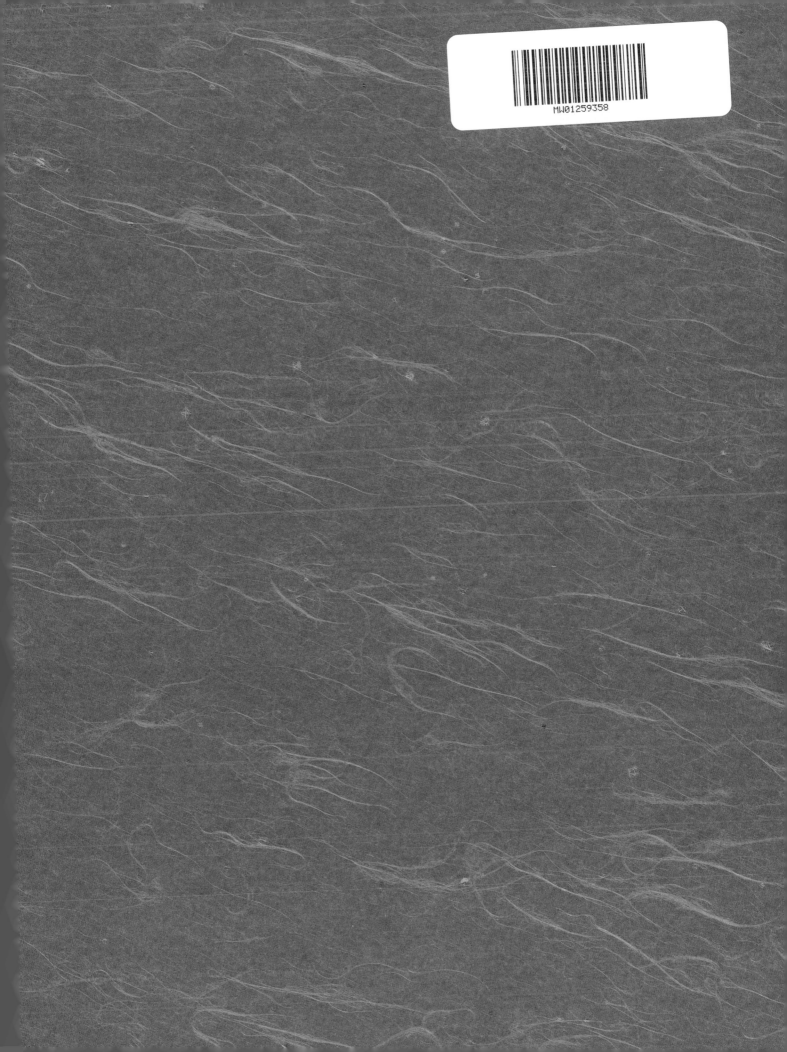

B-24 Liberators of the 15th Air Force/49th Bomb Wing

B-24 Liberators
of the
15th Air Force/49th Bomb Wing
in World War II

Michael D. Hill and John R. Beitling

Schiffer Military History
Atglen, PA

Acknowledgments

No one can undertake a project such as this without the help of numerous individuals. Bob and I are grateful for the help of the following, who opened their files and helped supply information for this undertaking: Glenn Strong, Allen Blue, Wally Forman, Robert Dorr, Glenn Strong, Jon and Pam Moran (461st), William Bloom (484th), Robert Blair (451st), Harry Helyer (451st), Joe Garde (451st), Julius Altvater (451st), Robert Taylor (451st), Lewis Williams (451st), George Tudor (451st), John Winden (451st), Peter Marioles (451st), Fred Kalinka (451st), Rev Paul Johnshoy (451st), Gordon Snyder (451st), Thomas "Doc" Moran (451st), Karl Eichhorn (451st), Harvey Clapp (451st), Douglas Wadlund (451st), Walter Stewart (484th), Don James (461st), Ted Wise (461st), Pat Roy (461st), Wayne Boyce (461st), Tom Moss (461st), George Leffler (461st), Rick Smith (461st), Len Cole (461st), and Stan Staples (461st).

Special THANKS to Bud Markel from the 484th Bomb Group Association for the loan of photos and permission to use material from newsletters and their website. We also thank Hughes Glantzberg for his help and permission to use material from the 461st Bomb Group website. A Special mention goes to Robert Karstensen for writing our foreword and providing special material for the 451st Bomb Group.

Bob mentions a "special" thanks to his wife, Carol, for her support during his years of research on the B-24 Liberator.

I give special Thanks to my family, Sedgefield and Wilda Hill, for the support that only parents can give. Finally, my wife Linda, for all of her loving support in my writing projects.

With the daily shrinking of ranks of the World War II veterans, Bob and I dedicate this work to all of the men who flew, repaired, and worked with the B-24s of the 15th Air Force's 49th Bomb Wing.

Book Design by Ian Robertson.

Printed in China.
ISBN: 0-7643-2343-3

We are interested in hearing from authors with book ideas on related topics.

Published by Schiffer Publishing Ltd.
4880 Lower Valley Road
Atglen, PA 19310
Phone: (610) 593-1777
FAX: (610) 593-2002
E-mail: Info@schifferbooks.com.
Visit our web site at: www.schifferbooks.com
Please write for a free catalog.
This book may be purchased from the publisher.
Please include $3.95 postage.
Try your bookstore first.

In Europe, Schiffer books are distributed by:
Bushwood Books
6 Marksbury Avenue
Kew Gardens
Surrey TW9 4JF
England
Phone: 44 (0) 20 8392-8585
FAX: 44 (0) 20 8392-9876
E-mail: Info@bushwoodbooks.co.uk.
Free postage in the UK. Europe: air mail at cost.
Try your bookstore first.

Contents

Foreword:

When the authors, Mike Hill and Bob Beitling, contacted me to write a foreword to this book, I was truly caught off guard. My literary experience encompasses some writing/reporting for a small local hometown newspaper, of which they knew nothing, and most recently doing a newsletter for the 451st Bomb Group called "Ad Lib." The Ad Lib is a spin-off from the old Base flyer that told about happenings on the Castelluccio Air Field during our wartime tenure. Apart from that, I had questions as to "Why me?"

But, the more I pondered the subject, the more I came to realize that they were looking for someone that had experienced the trauma that comes with high altitude combat flying. They were not looking for a big-time hero, nor were they looking for someone that was barely familiar with the B-24. They were seeking someone that could relate to what it was like to fly in the B-24, and to have seen combat first hand.

In that sense I qualified with my 389 hours of B-24 flying time. Our crew (Captain Henry G. Rollins' crew, 724th Bomb Squadron) completed our tour of 35 combat missions; Pilot and Engineer awarded the Distinguished Flying Cross; and five of us garnered the Purple Heart. This including our Radio Operator, T/Sgt Anthony Paonessa, who was killed in action on 29 December 1944. We were also entitled to wear nine Battle Stars on our Campaign Ribbon, plus three Distinguished Unit Citations. Those facts did not make us an exemplary crew, but I would place us as about average for the 10 months we were in a combat zone, starting in late June 1944. There were some crews that came through the war totally unscathed, while others made the supreme sacrifice.

It was unique that, during our 10 months overseas and through the course of 35 missions we, flying as a crew, or separately, flew many of our missions in a variety of B-24 aircraft of the 451st. This was due to our pilot being elevated to Squadron Operations Officer, and mostly flying with other pilots in lead positions. We, the rest of the crew, were relegated to flying as ìsparesî with other crews.

Early on, the original crews flew most of their missions in the same aircraft they brought overseas. But it was most uncommon for the later crews to have flown all your missions in one-only aircraft. If ìyourî aircraftóthe one you may have named or felt most attached toówas down for repair and the next mission called for

ìmaximum effort,î you flew whatever was available. Thus, many of the 724th Bomb Squadron aircraft listed in this book were familiar to me.

Sometimes, if you were flying ìlead,î it may be that your aircraft came from one of the other Squadrons (e.g., Radar (Mickey) Ship, or one with a newer version Bombsight).

I cannot conclude this foreword without putting in something about the B-24, and some of the hardships that the crewmen endured. One, seldom mentioned, was the cold. Flying between 20,000 and 25,000 feet altitude the temperature could reach between 40 to 60 degrees below zero. Protected only by an electrically heated suit (jacket, trousers, gloves, and boots), it was sometimes difficult to keep warm, especially in the waist section with open waist windows. In case of a malfunction with gun or equipment, you wore a pair of silk gloves, so when the heated outer gloves were removed you didn't become attached/frozen to any metal. Turrets could be uncomfortable because of close confinement, plus lack of motion that could help in circulating the blood in the lower extremities.

Oxygen masks were worn above 10,000 feet, and there were times when they froze, causing much distress by the wearer.

Flak Vests were considered mandatory in combat, as were the parachutes. The crewman was responsible for his own parachute, but the Engineer was accountable for the flak vests being on board prior to take-off. The flak vests were flexible two piece (front and back), supposedly bullet and shrapnel proof protectors. At altitude it usually required yourself and someone else to put on prior to going over the target. In emergency it only took a tug of a short lanyard to rid yourself of them.

Parachutes came in a variety of types. There were ìseat,î ìback,î and ìchest chutes.î Most common among the gunners was the chest chute. These were not worn until an emergency arose, and were placed in a position, within the aircraft, that was easily accessible when, and if, that emergency should happen. While the seat and back chutes were ready at all times, the chest chute had to be attached by way of metal snaps that were on the harness. This fact caused some concern, in the way that it could not be worn beneath the flak vest. Another factor was that if the aircraft suffered severe turbulence, either by flak damage or evasive action, you may be spending precious moments trying to relocate your chute where you left it.

There was another hazard faced by a crewman while on a mission. That was to see your wingman or buddy falling out of formation, and trying to follow what was happening to the aircraft. Maybe they would make it home, or maybe you would see them bailout, or worse yet—explode. Of course, this wasn't a physical hazard, but rather an emotional one.

It seems that history and research sometimes go hand in hand. When history is made, and allowed to become faded with time, then research comes into play to bring it back into focus. Thus will be the purpose of this book.

The 49th Wing of the 15th Army Air Force was once a mighty military force that the Allies had, and used effectively, to defeat the Nazis in WW II. And our weapon was the B-24 Liberator bomber. To the veteran and researcher alike, this book will be a great tool in bringing sharper focus to that part of history and to WW II.

Former S/Sgt Robert Karstensen (Gunner),
15th AAF, 49th Bombardment Wing,
451st Bomb Group, 724th Bomb Squadron.

Introduction

Sitting on the ground the B-24 Liberator appeared to be a designer's nightmare. She had long thin tapered wings attached to a slab sided fuselage. The wings did not look like they would support the weight in-flight, and the fuselage cried out for garish nose art adornment. Add to this two oval rudders, and one would think that she wouldn't get off the ground. But get off the ground she did! Once she was in the air, the long wings flexed upward to support the aircraft, and she assumed a grace all her own.

Built in more numbers than any other American bomber of World War II, the Liberator was the most advanced heavy bomber until surpassed by the B-29 Superfortress. She was overshadowed by the B-17 Flying Fortress through no fault of her own.

It was merely a matter of public relations. Used by the 8th Air Force, she was saddled with a bad reputation based on losses sustained during operations against Hitler's Germany. This reputation was in large part based on the fact that the 8th Air Force was primarily a B-17 Air Force. In most cases the Liberator units were forced to fly missions behind the B-17 units. Since the B-24 had a higher airspeed they would have to hold back in order to stay with the formations. This placed the Liberator at a severe operational disadvantage.

The 15th Air Force was made up of 21 heavy bomber groups, of which 15 groups were equipped with the B-24 Liberator. In this area of operations the B-24 was not hindered by the performance differences between the B-17 and the Liberator. In most cases the missions were planned and assigned to the groups to optimize the capabilities of each bomber type.

There has always been the great ìbomber debateî as to which aircraft was better, the B-17 or the B-24. It is not our purpose to enter into this abyss, as there is no concrete answer. If one looks strictly at the performance envelope of the aircraft the B-24 would come out as the better of the two. We must remember that each of these great aircraft had certain differences in construction, armament, and flight characteristics that would give them the advantage under different circumstances. It is only the authorsí place to say that if either of these planes brought you back from the flak filled skies of Europe, then she was ìthe best.î

When the idea for this project was put forth, I could think of no one to bring onboard other than John ìBobî Beitling. He is no stranger to B-24 researchers. He has spent over 20 years researching the B-24 Liberator. Bobís interest in the B-24 is natural; he flew as a crew member on the Liberator with the 389th Bomb Group in England during the war. Bob has helped me on several other projects dealing with the B-24, and I am proud and happy to have him as my copilot on this one.

My interest in the Liberator comes from the fact that my dad served with the 451st Bomb Group, 15th Air Force during the war. As a boy, I loved looking at his fading photos from that time. As a result I became a ìplane person,î and my interest in the Liberator has never faded.

So much has been written about the aircraft of World War II. In many cases, a certain aircraft is mentioned in these writings regarding the fact that it was lost on a certain date, or that it carried a certain name. Bob and I have used a different format. Our idea is to concentrate on the aircraft itself and give a biographical history of the individual aircraft. With that in mind, we are presenting as much information as possible about these historic Liberators. We have tried to include such things as her nickname and how she was named, mission history, and her eventual fate. We have also tried to include any interesting incidents that she was involved in. We hope that this different approach will serve as an important addition to the historical documentation of what not only the crews, but these aircraft, did for our countrieís history.

We have made every attempt to insure that the material that we present is as accurate as possible. We admit that with the passage of time, as well as the problems with record keeping of that time, add to some of the dilemmas presented in historical research. With that in mind, Bob and I hope that you enjoy our work and find it interesting.

History of the 49ᵗʰ Bomb Wing

Constituted as the 49th Bombardment Operational Training Wing (medium) on March 17, 1943, it was activated on March 31, 1943, at Columbia Army Air Base, Columbia, South Carolina. The Wing was transferred to Greenville, South Carolina, in April 1943, and remained there until February 1944. The primary mission was training of aircrews for service overseas.

In April 1944 the 49th Bomb Wing was reassigned to the 15th Air Force operating in Italy. The Wing was transferred without aircraft to Italy.

After being assigned to the 15th Air Force, the 451st Bomb Group was transferred from the 47th Wing, and the 461st was transferred from the 55th Wing. The newly arrived 484th Bomb Group was assigned as the last group in the wing. Most wings were composed of four Bomb Groups. Since the 49th was the last Wing using the B-24 assigned to the 15th—they were unique in the fact that the wing was comprised of only three Bomb Groups. The groups assigned to the Wing were the 451st, 461st, and 484th Bomb Groups.

The 49th Wing under the command of Brig/General William Lee moved into their headquarters near Foggia, Italy, and conducted Wing Operations for the duration of World War II.

The 49th Bomb Wing was inactivated in Italy on October 16, 1945. It was later redesignated as the 49th Bombard Wing (Very Heavy) and transferred to the reserve. Activated again on December 26, 1946, it had a short period of service until being deactivated again on June 27, 1949.

One November 7, 1951, it was redesignated as the 49th Air Division and assigned to the Tactical Air Command. In April 1952 it was transferred to England as part of the United States Air Force in Europe.

1

451ˢᵗ Bomb Group

History of the 451st Bomb Group

The 451st Bomb Group was activated under provisions of General Order # 5, paragraph 1 at Davis Monthan Field, Tucson, Arizona, on April 22, 1943. This order activated the group with four squadrons, the 724th, 725th, 726th, and 727th. The group would be under the command of Colonel Robert E.L. Eaton.

The group was transferred to Wendover Field, Utah, to begin training for combat. The major problem with Wendover was that there were several groups stationed there, and it was overcrowded.

In September 1943 the group was transferred to Fairmont Field, Nebraska. Located about 75 miles southwest of Lincoln, the group would remain there and complete their stateside training.

Orders were cut in November proclaiming the group ready for movement to their combat area. The aircrews began the flight to Italy in November 1943, while the ground echelon boarded trains for the East coast and their long boat ride across the Atlantic.

The ground echelon was reunited on January 2, 1944, at their first operational base at Gioia del Colle, Italy. On January 20, 1944, the air echelon arrived, and preparations were begun for the groupís first mission.

On arrival the 451st Bomb Group had been assigned to the 47th Bomb Wing. This wing was made up of the 98th, 376th, 449th, and 450th Bomb Groups. With the addition of the 451st, the 47th wing had five bomb groups assigned to it.

The 451st flew its first combat mission on January 30, 1944. Their target was the Radar Station at Fier, Albania. Like all groups on their first mission, it was fouled up from the beginning.

By March 1944 the base at Gioia del Colle was deemed unfit for combat operations due to mud and water. The group was split into two parts. The 724th and 726th Bomb Squadrons were transferred to San Pancrazio. The 725th and 727th were sent to Manduria. The group would operate from the two different bases until their new base was operational.

On April 6, 1944, the 451st began its movement to their new base at Castelluccia, Italy. With this movement also came the transfer to the newly activated 49th Bomb Wing.

The 451st continued to fly combat missions from their new base during the summer of 1944. They racked up missions to Ploesti, Vienna, and other targets in the Third Reich.

Like other groups in the 15th Air Force, the 451st was taking losses and getting replacements. August saw the group flying a devastating mission to Markersdorf, Austria. For this mission the group was awarded an unprecedented third Distinguished Unit Citation.

During the fall and winter of 1944-1945, the 451st continued to fly when the weather permitted. While the German Luftwaffe had been subdued, flak was always a threat.

On April 26, 1945, the 451st flew their 245th mission since arriving in Italy. It was to be the last mission flown by the group in World War II.

Shortly victory in Europe was proclaimed, and the men of the 451st began looking forward to returning to the United States.

During combat service in Italy the 451st was awarded three Distinguished Unit Citations. The first was awarded for the mission to Regansburg, Germany, on February 25, 1944. The second was awarded for the April 5, 1944, mission to Ploesti, Rumania. The final DUC was awarded for the August 23, 1944, mission to Markersdorf, Austria. It is noted that no other group was awarded three Unit Citations while in service with the 15th Air Force.

During the history of the 451st in World War II there were three commanding officers. Colonel Robert E.L. Eaton was the first commander, serving from activation until he completed 50 missions. Colonel James B Knapp took command of the group on September 19, 1944, and commanded until December when he gave command to Colonel Leroy Stefonowicz (Stefon), who commanded the group until the end of the war.

The 451st was reactivated for a brief time as a Stategic Missile Wing, and stood nuclear alert with the Strategic Air Command until being deactivated.

Aircraft and Markings

The original Liberators of the 451st were all B-24H models. The aircraft arrived in the olive drab and neutral gray factory finish. As replacements arrived the group soon owned a variety of different B-24 models.

On arrival in Italy the group was assigned to the 47th Bomb Wing. At this time the 47th Wing's tail markings were a white circle with a triangle painted within. These markings were painted on the vertical stabilizer. The 451st was the fifth group in the wing, and had a white circle with the number 5 painted on the lower half of the vertical stabilizer.

On transfer to the new 49th Bomb Wing the markings changed. A white circle with a red hexagon was painted on the upper stabilizer. A white circle with a red number one was painted on the lower half. To help quickly identify the group the middle part of the rudder was painted white.

These markings were shortly changed to the evolving 49th tail markings. This consisted of the upper half of the vertical stabilizer being painted red. The group marking for the 451st was a large red circle painted on the lower half of the vertical stabilizer. The horizontal stabilizer was also painted in the basic style at first, with later markings showing the entire unit being painted red.

As with the groups of the 15th Air Force, each aircraft was assigned an identification insignia. The 451st painted large numbers on the sides of the forward and rear fuselage. These numbers have been called ìbattle numbers,î or ìplane in groupî number. Recent research has shown that in most cases these numbers also corresponded to the revetment number that the aircraft had been assigned. The size of these numbers varied somewhat from group to group. To help identify the aircraftís squadron these were usually painted in squadron colors. The 724th used a large black rectangle with white numbers, while the 725th used red for their background, and the 726th used green for their background. The 727th squadron color was yellow, so aircraft of this squadron sported a yellow rectangle with red numbers to identify their aircraft.

As time past, many of the groupís aircraft also had their cowling rings painted in squadron colors. Several even went so far as to paint the propeller hubs in squadron colors.

Most of the original aircraft carried some type of nose art or name painted on the side of the aircraft. Nose art was very common, and varied depending on the crews and groundcrews that were assigned to the aircraft.

Liberators of the 451st Bomb Group

41-23733 SKIPPER-THE TUNERVILLE TROLLEY

This was the only known B-24D to serve with the 451st while overseas. She departed the USA on December 5, 1942, and was assigned to the 98th BG. She had a long combat history with the 98th. Her most notable mission was the low level mission to Ploesti on August 1, 1943; she aborted that mission with mechanical problems. She was declared unfit for combat in June 1944. She was transferred to the 724th Bomb Squadron (451st) and became a "steak and eggs" ship. She had flown 125 missions during her combat service.

41-28614 CRATER MAKER (727th #14)

Departed the USA on December 10, 1943, with Marshall Coulter and Crew #70 as an original aircraft to the group. She flew 64 known missions and was salvaged on August 22, 1944.

41-28680 (724th)

An original group aircraft of the 461st Bomb Group. During her service with the 461st she was known as TEN ACES AND A QUEEN. Transferred to the 47th Bomb Wing on February 28, 1944. The aircraft was assigned to the 451st shortly after arriving at the 47th Wing. Crashed and exploded on take off on March 23, 1944. Wilbert Sunmann and the crew were killed in the accident. (ACCIDENT REPORT 44-3-23-502)

41-23733 SKIPPER-THE TUNERVILLE TROLLEY

41 28614 CRATER MAKER

41-28804 SPECIAL MISSION

41-28740 RHODA (725th)
Originally assigned to the 461st BG, she departed the USA on February 1, 1944, where she was known as THE BAT. Transferred to the 451st, she was lost on the mission to Zagreb, Yugoslavia, on April 12, 1944, with the crew of R.W. Bergman (MACR #4192).

41-28760 SPECIAL DELIVERY (726TH #63 &#75)
Departed the USA on February 25, 1944, she was assigned to the 451st as a radar "Mickey Ship." On August 20, 1944, she was forced to land at Foggia Main due to battle damage. She was repaired, and returned to the group on October 15, 1944. She was transferred to Depot 52 on March 13, 1945, and believed salvaged. This B-24 was also known as MISS JO ANN.

41-28786 DIDDLIN DOLLY II (724th)
Departed the USA on March 24, 1944. Assigned to the group in May 1944 to replace 44-52077.

41-28804 SPECIAL MISSION (727th #63 & #75)
Departed the USA April 20, 1944. Assigned to the group as a Mickey Ship in June 1944. This aircraft crashed on September 12, 1944.

41-28806 LITTLE DE-ICER (725TH)
Departed the USA on March 24, 1944. This aircraft was condemned on May 5, 1944.

41-28806 LITTLE DE-ICER

41-28816 SCRAPPY

41-28816 SCRAPPY (725th #57)
Departed the USA on March 20, 1944. She was flown overseas by Crew #30, commanded by Joseph Younger. SCAPPY was lost on Mission 108 to Vienna. R.L. Worsthorn and his crew were able to bail out. (MACR # 8005)

41-28860 T.S. THE CHAPLIN (726th #51)
Departed the USA on May 20, 1944. This aircraft was assigned to the 484th Bomb Group as a radar "Mickey Ship." She was transferred to the 451st on October 10, 1944. Believed to have been returned to the USA after the war. Her crew chief was Robert McGee

41-28860 T.S. THE CHAPLIN (center)

41-28861 BURMA BOUND

41-28861 BURMA BOUND (725th #69 & 74)
This radar Mickey Ship departed the USA on May 29, 1944, and was assigned to the 451st in June 1944. On July 29, 1944, she was transferred to the 461st for a brief time, then returned to the 451st. On October 7, 1944, she was badly damaged by flak on Mission #130. Pilot George Tudor was able to make an emergency landing at Vis. On this mission Squadron Commander Major Dooley was seriously wounded. For bringing the crippled ship home, George Tudor was awarded the Silver Star. The aircraft was repaired and returned to Depot 52 for major repairs. BURMA BOUND returned to the 451st on November 25, 1944, and completed the war, returning to the USA .

41-28862 (727th)
Departed the USA on May 15, 1944, assigned to the 451st on September 11, 1944. This Mickey Ship crashed at base on February 14, 1945.

41-28876 NICKLE PLATE CRATE (727TH #8)
Departed the USA on March 24, 1944, and assigned to the 451st in June. Sustained a direct flak hit on the nose turret on July 3, 1944, killing the nose gunner, Donald Outman. The damage was repaired. On September 15, 1944, the nose wheel was damaged on landing the aircraft was deemed unfit for combat, and was salvaged on November 30, 1944.

41-28897 MIDNIGHT MICKEY (725th # 75 & 58)
A radar Mickey Ship, this aircraft departed the USA on June 16, 1944, and was assigned to the 451st in July. She survived the war, and returned to the ZI on June 10, 1945.

41-28876 NICKLE PLATE CRATE

41-28897 MIDNIGHT MICKEY

41-28931 TíINGS IS TUFF

41-28933 FERP FINESCO

41-28931 T'INGS IS TUFF (727th #28)

Left the USA on April 27, 1944, with the crew of Douglas Wadlund. Arrived in May, and was assigned to the 451st. Crash-landed on May 14, 1944, and was sent to Depot 52. In July she returned to the group, and was assigned to the 724th SQ. On August 17, 1944 (Mission #105), she was badly damaged by flak over Ploesti. The crew was able to make it back and crash-landed at the base. It is noted that an Army Air Force film crew was at the base and captured the landing on film. The crew was able to walk away from the plane, but she was deemed unfit for repair and salvaged on August 18, 1944.

41-28933 FERP FINESCO (725TH #38)

Departed the USA on April 4, 1944, and was assigned to the 451st in June 1944. Name derived from the first letter of the crew's home town name. Lost to flak on Mission #92, July 28, 1944, to Ploesti, with the crew of Glenn Kerres (MACR #7060).

41-28950 WOLF WAGON II (724TH #18)

Departed the USA on April 18, 1944, and was assigned to the group to replace John O'Conner's original WOLF WAGON on April 25, 1944. Crew Chief Frank Baird kept her ready to fly. Lost to flak on July 28, 1944, with the crew of Robert Duncan (MACR #7041).

41-28955 KLUNKER (726TH #36)

Left the USA on April 16, 1944, and was originally assigned to the 725th. Transferred to the 726th in August. Listed as MIA on October 13, 1944, she actually had landed at VIS. She was repaired and returned to the group on November 5, 1944. Flown by William Jackson's crew on November 17, 1944. KLUNKER was lost due to fuel starvation due to battle damage (MACR #9884).

41-28957 BIGGER BOOBER GIRL (727th #13)

Left the USA on April 16, 1944, and arrived in May to replace BIG BOOBER GIRL. On May 14, 1944, while flying her third mission she was badly damaged, and crash-landed at the base with two crewmen wounded. Her pilot that day was Roger Sprowles. She was towed to the scrap yard and salvaged.

41-28950 WOLF WAGON II

41-28957 BIGGER BOOBER GIRL

41-29175 PISTOL PACKIN MAMA

41-29175 PISTOL PACKIN MAMMA (724TH)
This original group aircraft departed the USA on November 30, 1943, with Crew # 4 under the command of Clifford Kester. She made a crash landing at Gioia del Cole on February 2, 1944, due to a flak punctured tire.

41-29194 SHACK ? WOLF! (725TH)
An original group ship, she departed the USA on December 2, 1943, with Crew #21 under the command of Edward L. Wilson. She was transferred to the 449th BG in February, and was lost with that group on February 25th.

41-29195 GASHOUSE (724th)
Delivered to the group at Fairmont, Nebraska, and was assigned to Robert Stone's crew #3. During a training mission a fuel connection came loose, spilling over 200 gallons of fuel into the bomb bay. From that day on she was known as GASHOUSE. On May 8, 1944, a short circuit caused an uncontrollable fire to erupt. Crew Chief Walter Flannally and his ground crew fought the fire, but the plane finally exploded and burned at the hard stand.

41-29194 SHACK? WOLF!

GASHOUSE

41-29199 BIG BOOBER GIRL

41-29209 HOP SCOTCH

41-29219 BOOMERANG

41-29199 BIG BOOBER GIRL(727th)

This original group ship left the USA on December 7, 1943, with Crew #56 under the command of Roger G. Sprowles. Her Crew Chief was Doug Holmes. Listed as MIA on Mission #34 to Bucharest on April 24, 1944, with the crew of Forest Jones. The crew managed to bail out over Yugoslavia and evade capture.

41-29209 HOP SCOTCH (727th #17)

This original 727th aircraft was named after a training mission. Crew #62, commanded by Wilfred McAllister, stopped at Pierre, South Dakota, for an overnight stay. While in town they stopped at the Hop Scotch bar in downtown Pierre. The owner of the bar said he would give them a case of Scotch if they would name their B-24 after his bar. The plane was named, and the crew got the Scotch. She departed the USA December 7, 1943, and was one of the last group aircraft to arrive in Italy. She had a reputation as being a problem ship, but her Crew Chief, Joe Garde, kept her mission ready. On May 19, 1944, HOP SCOTCH aborted the mission due to oil pressure loss on the #1 engine. Returning to their base, Pilot Edward Hook made a hard landing with a full load of fuel and bombs. One of the bombs came loose from the shackle and fell through the bomb bay doors, following HOP SCOTCH down the runway. It did not explode. Thus, HOP SCOTCH has the distinction of bombing her own air base. During refueling she caught fire on August 20, 1944. Although the fire was put out, she was condemned and transferred to Depot 52.

41-29219 BOOMERANG (725th #30)

An original aircraft of the group, she departed the USA on December 7, 1943, with Crew #27, under the command of John P. Janensch. She flew 69 known missions, and was credited with four enemy fighters when she was salvaged due to battle damage on September 23, 1943.

41-29426 CITADEL (725th)

Departed the USA with the 484th Bomb Group. She was assigned to the 451st in July 1944. Sustained major flak damage on September 9, 1944, and was sent to Deport 52 for repair. She returned to duty with the 451st on October 1, 1944. Crashed at the 451st's base on December 15, 1944.

41-29220 NAUGHTY BUT NICE aka HONEY CHILD (725th)

An original aircraft of the group, she departed the USA on December 2, 1943, under the command of James G. Price and Crew #25. She was listed as MIA on April 17, 1944, during the group's 29th mission. Sustained two flak hits near Mostar, Yugoslavia. Left formation and headed down. Three of the crew, commanded by James Price, bailed out (MACR # 4078).

41-29229 OZARK UPSTART /OLD TUB (726th #56 & 45)

Departed the USA on December 7, 1943. An original group aircraft, she was flown overseas by Crew #51, under the command of Janes Hunt. She was transferred to Depot 52 on July 13, 1944, and believed salvaged. She flew 41 known missions.

41-29229 OZARK UPSTART (OLD TUB)

41-29233 THE SOD BUSTER

41-29233 THE SOD BUSTER (727th #15)

An original group aircraft, she departed the USA under the command of Cortland Reed and his Crew #64 on December 13, 1943. After each mission the ground crew would paint a small plowshare instead of a bomb to denote her missions. She flew 60 missions without aborting due to mechanical problems. Her Crew Chief, Albert Kvorjak, always kept her in the best condition. He was awarded the Bronze Star for his effort. On April 17, 1944, she returned from the mission with over 200 holes in her skin. With over 69 plowshares and five enemy fighters to her credit she was salvaged on September 20, 1944.

41-29238 SUSAN DIANE (727th #11)

This original group aircraft departed the USA on December 7, 1943, under the command of Arthur Foremanek and Crew #59. After sustaining major battle damage on Mission #81, July 14, 1944, she was declared Class 26 and salvaged.

41-29239 SHILAY-LEE (727th #4)

She departed the USA on December 10, 1943, as part of the original cadre under the command of Francis "Mike" Boyle and Crew #68. Her Crew Chief was Harry Steinberg. Instead of bombs to denote missions, small clubs were painted on her. On May 5, 1944 (Mission #38), to Ploesti, the aircraft was damaged by flak in the left wing root. The #2 engine was shot out, and the landing gear had dropped from the wheel well. On the flight deck, Mike Boyle had been wounded by flak. Co-pilot Samuel Moore had been killed by flak. Francis "Mike" Boyle ordered the crew to bail out. Although badly wounded, Boyle held the ship level long enough for the crew to escape. Before he could jump SHILAY-LEE exploded. He was awarded the Distinguished Service Cross for his action (MACR # 5446), the highest award for the group. At the time of her loss she had flown 30 missions.

41-29238 SUSAN DIANE

41-29239 SHILAY-LEE

41-29241 ROYAL PROD

41-29241 ROYAL PROD (727th #12)

Merle Larson and crew departed the USA on December 11, 1943, as part of the original cadre, with Crew #67 commanded by Merle Larson. Her Crew Chief was Robert Pratt. After a long combat career ROYAL PROD was deemed unfit for combat and became a "steak and eggs" ship. She was returned to the USA on June 9, 1945.

41-29242 FLABBERGASTED FANNY (726th #46)

Departing the USA on December 7, 1943, under the command of Lester Snyder and Crew #50, she was an original group aircraft. On 12 September, while flying her 47th mission, she was listed as MIA. The aircraft hand landed at VIS and returned late. Due to battle damage she was salvaged on September 20, 1944.

41-29244 DOUBLE TROUBLE (725th)

Departed the USA on December 2, 1943, as an original group aircraft. On February 25, 1944, she was attacked by enemy fighters. The #4 engine was shot out, and DOUBLE TROUBLE lagged behind the formation. The fighters attacked the cripple. Six parachutes were observed. It was also observed that the tail gunner remained in his turret and dueled with the fighters on the way down. She was flown that day by the crew commanded by Edwin Pries.

41-29245 (725th)

Departed the USA on December 2, 1943, with Crew #28, commanded by Kenneth Morse. Lost to fighter attacks over Steyr, Austria, on April 2, 1944, with Frank Howard's crew (MACR #3718).

4129242 FLABBERGASTED FANNY

41-29244 DOUBLE TROUBLE (front)

41-29253 EASY DOES IT

41-29251 SHE HASTA/IMPATIENT VIRGIN (724TH)
Departed the USA on December 2, 1943, under the command of Robert Nagel with Crew #13. Lost to fighter attacks on June 11, 1944, on Mission #64, with the crew of Charles Haun (MACR # 5668).

41-29253 EASY DOES IT (724th #26)
Departed the USA on December 2, 1943, as part of the original group, with Crew #13, under the command of John Kearney. Her original crew chief at Fairmont, Nebraska, was Walter Cutchin. She crash-landed at Castelluccio during a practice mission. The aircraft stalled during landing and blew all three tires. She flew 42 known missions.

41-29256 SAKINSHACK (724th #23)
An original group aircraft, she departed the USA on December 17, 1943, with crew #12, under the command of Robert James. She was dropped from the group records on September 20, 1944.

41-29258 SATAN'S SISTER (724th)
An original aircraft, departed the USA on December 6, 1943, with Crew #10, under the command of Thomas Moran. Later renamed MAIRZY DOATS. She was transferred to the 449th Bomb Group shortly after arriving in Italy. She was lost to enemy action on April 4, 1944, with the 449th. Her 451st crew chief was Glen Swearingen.

41-29256 SAKINSHACK

41-29490 GEMINI

41-29490 GEMINI(725th #35)
Transferred from the 486th Bomb Group of the 8th Air Force, known as the Zodiacs. She arrived on February 8, 1945, to replace 44-48774. After several missions she was transferred to the 460th Bomb Group.

41-29530 AMERICAN BEAUTY (724TH #25)
Originally assigned to the 484th Bomb Group, she departed the USA on March 18, 1944. After transfer to the 451st she was listed MIA on June 23, 1944, on Mission #68 to Giurgiu, Romania. Commanded by Charles McCutchen on that mission. One of the crew was killed in action, and nine crewmen became POWs. (MACR #10720) Her Crew Chief was Philip Beckwith.

41-29530 AMERICAN BEAUTY

41-29541 PEACE TERMS

41-29541 PEACE TERMS/ICE COLD KATIE II (726th #47)
Departed the USA on March 24, 1944. Listed as MIA on July 28, 1944, on Mission #92 to Ploesti. The crew of Jack Holtz was able to escape the aircraft and became POWs (MACR #7036).

41-29580 SCREAMIN MEEMIE II (726th #55) Departed the USA on April 3, 1944. Damaged by enemy action on Mission #108 to Vienna on August 22, 1944. As far as can be determined the crew flew the aircraft back to the base and bailed out.

41-29590 FORD'S MISTAKE (725th #70)
Departed the USA on April 6, 1944. Assigned to the 451st in June 1944. Made a crash landing on June 25, 1944, the aircraft was repaired and transferred to the 449th Bomb Group.

42-50298 DIRTY GERTIE (727TH #7)
Departed the USA on April 28, 1944. MIA on August 17, 1944, on Mission #105 to Ploesti. After sustaining battle damage the crew was able to bail out. (MACR # 07678).

42-50389 LITTLE BUTCH II (727TH #13 &#5)
Departed the USA on May 13, 1944. Assigned to the 451st in June as a replacement for the original LITTLE BUTCH. Sustained major flak damage on July 28, 1944, and sent to 60th SS for repair. Returned to duty on August 23, 1944. Ran out of fuel on December 18, 1944, on Mission #169 to Blechhammer with the crew of Harry Blank (MACR #10640).

42-50630 ROUND TRIP (727th)
This radar Mickey Ship departed the USA on July 5, 1944, after modifications at the St. Paul, Minnesota, center. Arrived on July 17, 1944, and flew first mission on July 19, 1944. Lost to enemy action on December 11, 1944, with the crew of Wallace Harris (726th). Two of the crew were killed in action (MACR #10392).

41-29580 SCREAMIN MEEMIE II

41-29426 THE CITADEL

42-50298 DIRTY GERTIE

42-50389 LITTLE BUTCH II

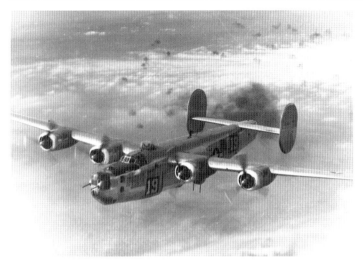

42-50906 MINNESOTA MAULER

42-50952 DAISEY MAE

42-50730 MUGLEY OTHER (727th)
This ex-8th AF aircraft arrived in the MTO on December 24, 1944. Assigned to the 451st on February 5, 1945. Sustained major flak damage on Mission #197, and was sent to the 60th S.S. Declared beyond repair and condemned on March 21, 1945.

42-50906 MINNESOTA MAULER (724th #19)
Departed the USA on July 10, 1944, and arrived on July 18, 1944. She replaced 42-78236 GAS HOUSE JR. Paul Johnshoy named her for his home state, and the fact that he wanted nothing to with any aircraft with the name GASHOUSE again. Her Crew Chief was John Cook. She was forced to land at Foggia Main on January 24, 1945, due to battle damage. She was repaired and returned to the group. Crash-landed with Fredrick Ade's crew at Zara, Yugoslavia, on March 9, 1945, due to battle damage, and was dropped from the group records.

42-50939 (727th)
Departed the USA on August 10, 1944. Made emergency landing at Vis on December 18, 1944, and returned to base the next day. On Mission #164, December 11, 1944, she sustained major damage over Munich. Lt. Wilson and crew managed to get the aircraft back to base, where most of the crew bailed out. Lt. Wilson and the Flight Engineer crash landed at the base. The aircraft was written off

42-50952 DAISY MAE (726th #48)
Departed the USA on July 7, 1944. Assigned to the 451st on August 6, 1944. Landed at Zara, Yugoslavia, on October 14, 1944, and later returned to the base. Made emergency landing at Vis due to damage on November 24, 1944, and returned on December 2, 1944. Sustained major flak damage on January 20, 1945, over Linz, Austria. She was transferred to Depot 52 on January 22, 1945.

42-51090 HEY MOE

42-51170 G.I. JILL

42-51222 IN THE MOOD

42-51090 HEY MOE aka LOIS M (725th #40)
Departed the USA on May 1, 1944. Assigned to the 451st in July. She flew 67 missions in 69 days. For this her Crew Chief, Gaylord Ault, was awarded the Bronze Star. She sustained flak damage to the left wing, which was repaired. On November 13th, returning from a "PX" flight to Bari, the pilot made a "hard" landing. On November 14, 1944, a new crew took her up for gunnery practice before flying their first combat mission. Just after take off the left wing buckled between #1 and #2 engines. HEY MOE crashed in a field, killing all 11 men on board. Records reveal that there were 288 hours and 50 minutes of flight time after the wing was repaired. It is believed that the hard landing may have caused the wing to become weakened, thus the subsequent failure.

41-51170 G.I. JILL (727th #62 & #4)
This ex-8th AF aircraft arrived in the MTO on January 6, 1945, and was assigned to the 451st on January 19, 1945, to replace 44-40578. She returned to the USA on June 6, 1945.

42-51222 IN THE MOOD (725th #56)
An ex-8th AF aircraft, she arrived in Italy on February 15, 1945. Assigned to the 451st on March 1, 1945, she was called IN THE MOOD, after the popular song. She survived the war and returned to the USA on June 5, 1945, under the command of John J. Mauer.

42-51271 #73

42-51297 HOT 2 TROT

41-51271 (724th #72)
An ex-8th AF Liberator, she arrived in the MTO on December 24, 1944. Assigned to the 451st on February 6, 1945. While taxing after landing the co-pilot made a left turn near the 727th area. The turn was short, and the aircraft went into a ditch off the taxi strip. Declared "Class 26" and salvaged on February 10, 1945.

42-51297 HOT 2 TROT (727TH #10)
Departed the USA on July 20, 1944, arriving at the 451st on August 6, 1944, to replace 44-64445 PATSY JACK. Ditched in the Adriatic on November 4, 1944.

42-51300 WET DREAM (726th #42)
Departed the USA on July 17, 1944, arriving at the 451st on July 23rd to replace 41-29229. Lost to enemy action on August 22, 1944. WET DREAM blew up over the target, killing three of the crew, commanded by Valerian Klein (MACR # 8002).

42-51306 (725th)
Left the USA on July 25, 1944. Assigned to the 451st on November 24, 1944, to replace 44-40623. Lost to enemy action on Mission #158 to Blechhammer on December 2, 1944. J.D. Eckersley and all but one of the crew escaped the aircraft (MACR #10034).

42-51300 WET DREAM

42 51314 HELL'S HEP CATS

42-51314 HELLS HEP CATS (724th #25 &#72)
Left the USA on July 17, 1944. Assigned to the 451st on July 22, 1944, to replace 42-52449. Alton Elliot was assigned as the aircraft's Crew Chief. Crash landed at Vis on November 5, 1944, and returned to base on December 1, 1944. Returned to the USA June 6, 1945.

42-51321 THE BAD PENNY (726th #49)
Departed the USA on July 20, 1944. Assigned to the 451st on July 30, 1944, to replace 42-52078. On Mission #142, November 1, 1944, to Vienna. THE BAD PENNY was hit by flak just after bombs away. The #3 and #4 fuel tanks were hit, causing fuel to be lost. #4 engine had to be shut down. Near Lake Ablation the plane was again hit by flak. The crew was able to pick up three P-51s as escort. Near the Drive River, two engines stopped due to fuel starvation. The crew of Rosser Bodycomb bailed out at 12,000 feet. The crew was able to evade capture, and returned to Allied control in January 1945 (MACR # 9585).

42-51334 KING HIGH (726TH #41)
Departed the USA on July 30, 1944. Arrived August 9, 1944. Flew first mission on August 23, 1944. On that mission to Markersdorf, she was attacked by fighters at 1206 hours. Cannon fire almost shot the entire tail away. KING HIGH fell about 3,000 feet from the formation before control was regained at about a 20 degree bank. After flying as far as they could Pilot Harvey Clapp had the crew bail out over the Island of Kirk, off the Yugoslavian coast. The crew was able to evade capture (MACR # 8326).

HELL'S HEP CATS

42-51321 THE BAD PENNY

42-51369 BOOT IN THE ASS

42-51337 (725th)
Departed the USA on July 18, 1944, arriving on August 7, 1944. Replaced 42-99754. Listed MIA on Mission #139, October 23, 1944. Flak damaged a fuel cell in the wing. Aircraft commander James Becklund left the formation, thinking the aircraft may explode. Aircraft ran out of fuel trying to return to base. All of the crew except Eugene Schwerdtfager managed to evade capture (MACR #9466).

42-51369 BOOT IN THE ASS (724TH #31)
Departed the USA on August 13, 1944, and was assigned to the 451st on August 30, 1944. On October 15, 1944, the right main landing gear collapsed due to material failure while under the command of Henry Rollins. The aircraft was repaired and returned to service. Crash-landed on Vis on November 5, 1944, and was declared Class 26.

42-51372 (725th)
Left the USA on August 11, 1944. Assigned to the 451st on December 12, 1944, to replace 42-51680. Sustained major flak damage on February 28, 1945. Aircraft was repaired and returned to service on 8 March. Crash-landed on March 9, 1945, and was sent to 60th S.S. for repair. Returned to active duty on March 22, 1945. Listed MIA after Mission #222 to Straszhof on March 25, 1945, with the crew of Mark Robinson (MACR # 13199).

42-51404 (724th)
Departed the USA on August 13, 1944. Assigned to the group on August 27, 1944, to replace 42-78523. This aircraft crash-landed at Vis on November 11, 1944, and returned to the group on December 4, 1944. Sustained major flak damage on December 25, 1944. Returned to the group on January 5, 1945. The aircraft returned to the USA after the war.

42-51360 #39

42-51564 FICKLE FINGER

42-51409 LUCKY TEN (727th)
LUCKY TEN left the USA on August 17, 1944, and was assigned to the group on September 9, 1944, to replace 42-28804. Albert Kvorjak was her Crew Chief. On Mission #130 to Vienna on October 7, 1944, she was lost to flak with the crew of Harvey Robinet. Five of the crew were KIA (MACR # 9024). At the time of her loss she had flown two missions.

42-51483 (726th)
Departed the USA on August 17, 1944, arriving with the group on September 21, 1944. Listed MIA after Mission #153 to Maribor on November 19, 1944. No record of a MACR.

42-51564 FICKLE FINGER (727th #16)
Departed the USA on September 24, 1944, to replace 44-40196. On Mission #134 to Vienna, October 13, 1944, she was hit by flak and went down, taking the entire crew of William Goin with her (MACR #9134).

42-51585 #52

42-51590 DESTINY'S TOTS

42-51585 (726th #52)
Departed the USA on August 11, 1944. Assigned to the group on August 24, 1944, to replace 42-5100. Listed as MIA on December 11, 1944. L.H. Porter and crew were able to bail out and return to base (MACR 10391).

42-51587 (726th)
Left the USA on August 18, 1944. Lost to flak on mission #134 to Vienna, October 13, 1944, with the crew of Ibar Spellacy. The crew evaded capture and returned to base (MACR 9056).

42-51590 DESTINY'S TOTS (724th #24)
Departed the USA on August 9, 1944. Assigned to the group to replace August 27, 1944, to replace 42-78165. Crashed near Bologna on April 24, 1945.

42-51616 (724th)
This radar Mickey Ship departed the USA on September 9, 1944. Assigned to the 451st on October 20, 1944, replacing 42-78647. Sustained major flak damage on December 26, 1944. She made it back to the base with over 100 holes in her. There were 13 flak holes in the nose turret alone. She was transferred for repair on January 1, 1945.

42-51626 #43

42-51674 BOTTOMS UP

42-51677 SKYLARK

42-51626 (726th #43)
Left the USA on August 8, 1944. Assigned to the group on September 21, 1944, to replace 42-78102. Sustained major flak damage on November 11, 1944. Made a crash landing at Foggia Main on December 18, 1944, and returned on January 19, 1945. Made emergency landing at Vis on February 1, 1945, returning on February 19, 1945. Returned to the USA on June 10, 1945.

42-51654 (725th) MICKEY FINNI
A radar Mickey Ship, she departed the USA on September 24, 1944. Assigned to the group on October 10, 1944, to replace 44-41060. Transferred on December 9, 1944, returning to the group on January 7, 1945. Returned to the USA on June 7, 1945.

42-51661 (725th)
Left the USA on August 17, 1944. Assigned to the group on September 20, 1944, to replace 41-29256. Lost on a non-operational accident on October 14, 1944. Sixteen men were killed when the aircraft crashed into a hillside near Rochetta, Italy.

42-51662 (726th #55 &42)
Departed the USA on August 20, 1944. Assigned to the group on September 21, 1944, to replace 42-51679. Crash-landed at Foggia Main on November 21, 1944. After repair she returned on January 11, 1945. After the war she returned to the USA on June 5, 1945.

42-51674 BOTTOMS UP (727th #8)
Left the USA on September 26, 1944. Assigned to the group on October 20, 1944. Sustained major flak damage on December 18, 1944. Returned to service on December 26, 1944. Damaged by flak again on December 29, 1944, she returned to combat on January 6, 1945. Returned to the USA on June 7, 1945.

42-51677 SKYLARK (726th #50)
Left the USA on August 23, 1944. Assigned to the group on October 15, 1944, to replace 42-52460. Sustained major flak damage on January 20, 1945. She was repaired and returned to service. Returned to the USA on June 3, 1945.

42-51680 WACO WENCH (SURF THING)

42-51747 #32

42-51750 GANG BANG

42-51679 (726th)
Departed the USA on August 12, 1944. Arrived on August 28, 1944, replacing 41-29580. Crashed on take off on September 3, 1944. The crew managed to escape as the ship caught fire off the end of the runway. The fire crews arrived and tried to fight the fire. The aircraft blew up about an hour later.

42-51680 WACO WENCH aka SURE THING (727th #11)
Departed the USA on August 16, 1944, and was originally assigned to the 726th Bomb Squadron. Transferred to the 727th. On November 11, 1944, she returned from the mission with severe battle damage. The crew bailed out over the base after heading the plane towards the Adriatic.

42-51682 BETTY JO (725th #35)
Left the USA on August 14, 1944. Assigned to the 725th on August 29, 1944, to replace THE EXTRA JOKER. Transferred to the 449th Bomb Group.

42-51729 (724th)
Left the USA on August 8, 1944. Assigned to the group on September 5, 1944. Listed MIA on August 23, 1944, after Mission #109 to Markersdorf, Austria. Lost to fighter attacks with the crew of Robert Beach (MACR 8253).

42-51732 (725th)
Departed the USA on August 24, 1944. Assigned to the group on September 21, 1944, she was transferred on September 30, 1944.

42-51874 LE PETITE FLEUR

42-51880 THE PURPLE SHAFT

42-51747 (725th #32)
Left the USA on August 15, 1944, arriving at the group on September 21, 1944, to replace 42-52440. On November 22, 1944, she spun out of control about an hour after take off, taking the crew with her. The cause of the crash was never determined.

42-51750 GANG BANG (727th #8)
Left the USA on August 11, 1944. Assigned to the group on September 1, 1944. Mike Thorrick was assigned as the Crew Chief. The impressive nose art was applied by Gordon Snyder. During a "trucking (supply) mission" to Lyons, France, on September 22, 1944, she was involved in a freak accident. During landing, she was struck in the left wing by a P-47 Thunderbolt that was taking off. The entire wing outboard of the #1 engine was ripped off. The crew escaped with bumps and bruises. The pilot of the Thunderbolt suffered a broken back. GANG BANG was classified Class 26 after her third mission.

42-51754 RABBIT HABIT (725th)
Departed the USA on August 18, 1944. Assigned to the group on September 6, 1944. Lost to flak on October 13, 1944. Five of the crew, commanded by Robert Baker, were killed in action (MACR #9047).

42-51872 DOTTY-DO (725th)
Departed the USA on August 28, 1944. Assigned to the group on October 1, 1944, and transferred to the 485th Bomb Group on October 9, 1944.

42-51874 LE PETITE FLEUR (727TH)
THE LITTLE FLOWER departed the USA on August 17, 1944, and arrived at the group on September 7, 1944. Sustained battle damage on Mission #154 to Blechhammer on November 20, 1944. Pilot Ed Doherty and crew were able to ditch the aircraft. They were picked up by Yugoslavian partisans and returned to Bari, Italy.

42-51980 #39

42-51984 MISS FIRE !!

42-51880 THE PURPLE SHAFT (724th #74)
Left the USA on September 3, 1944, and was assigned to the group on September 9, 1944. Listed MIA after Mission #176 to Udine, Italy, December 29, 1944. Took a direct flak hit near the target and exploded. Eight of the crew, under the command of Martin Uhl, were killed (MACR #10916).

42-51923 SHORT STUFF (725th)
Left the USA on September 24, 1944, and was assigned to the group on October 14, 1944. Destroyed by fire on the ground November 11, 1944.

42-51941 (726th #47)
Left the USA on September 21, 1944, arriving at the group on September 18, 1944. Listed as MIA after Mission #168 to Ordertal Oil Refinery on December 17, 1944. Involved in a mid-air collision with 42-52045 enroute to target. The entire crew of Theodore King were killed in the mishap (MACR #10682).

42-51947 (726th)
Departed the USA on September 8, 1944. Assigned to the group on October 13, 1944, to replace 42-51680 (WACO WENCH). Lost to flak on October 14, 1944, Mission #135 to Odertal Oil Refinery. The aircraft was commanded by Eugene Porter (MACR # 9150). The crew was able to escape the aircraft. This was the plane's first combat mission.

42-51960 (725th)
Left the USA on August 25, 1944. Assigned to the 451st on December 14, 1944, to replace 44-41114. Salvaged due to battle damage on February 27, 1945.

42-51970 (724th)
Left the USA on September 6, 1944. Assigned to the group on October 6, 1944, to replace 42-52099. Lost to flak on November 1, 1944, with the crew of E.L. Merritt. He and seven of his crew were killed (MACR #9584).

42-52036

42-52044 #14

42 51980 (725th)
Departed the USA on September 8, 1944. Assigned to the group on September 21, 1944, replacing 42-7475 (THUNDERMUG). Crashed on December 2, 1944.

42-51984 MISSFIRE!! (724th #22)
She left the USA on December 8, 1944. Assigned to the group on December 20, 1944, to replace 42-78580. Sustained major flak damage and declared Class 26 on December 26th.

42-51999 (725th)
Left the USA on September 28, 1944. Assigned to the group on October 17, 1944, replacing 42-51764. Sustained major flak damage December 2, 1944; was repaired and damaged again on December 17, 1944. Returned to the USA on June 7, 1945.

42 52036 (725th #54 & 43)
Departed the Zone of Interior (USA) on November 11, 1944. Assigned to the group on December 12, 1944, replacing 42-51306. Made emergency landing at Ibia on January 19, returning to base on January 30, 1945. Lost to a mid-air collision with 42-52440 (CALAMITY JANE) on February 7, 1945, with the crew of Darrell Burk (MACR #12090).

42-52044 (727th #14)
Left the USA on September 25, 1944. Assigned to the group on October 16, 1944, to replace 44-41152. Made emergency crash-landing at Bari on January 8, 1945, returning to the 451st on January 26, 1945. Returned to the USA on June 26, 1944.

42-52054 KNOCKERS UP

42-52045 (726th #36)
Left the USA on September 23, 1944. Assigned to the 451st on October 16th to replace 41-28955. Made an emergency landing on an island off Yugoslavia on November 7, 1944, and listed as MIA (MACR 9713). Returned to the group. On December 17, 1944, during mission #168, she was involved in a mid-air collision with 42-51941. The impact bent the left wing upward and tore the #1 engine off. Several of the crew bailed out shortly after the collision. After flying the stricken ship for several hours in an attempt to return to Italy, William Shelton and the remainder of the crew were able to bail out of the stricken aircraft over Yugoslavia (MACR #10681).

42-52047 (724th #29)
Left the USA on September 30, 1944. Crashed at the base on December 2, 1944. Sustained battle damage on Mission #158 to Blechhammer. The crew was able to fly the ship back to the base, where she made a spectacular crash-landing.

42-52054 KNOCKERS UP (727th #16)
She left the USA on September 22, 1944. Arrived on October 16, 1944, to replace 42-51564 (FICKLE FINGER). Lost to flak on Mission #201 to Linz, Austria, on February 25, 1945. Six of the crew, commanded by David Compton, were killed (MACR #12742).

42-52077 DIDDLIN DOLLY (724th)
Departed the USA on December 1, 1943, with Walter Graber's crew #5 as part of the original cadre of aircraft. Listed MIA on Mission #34, April 28, 1944. DIDDLIN DOLLY took a direct flak hit in the #2 engine and caught fire. Flown by Walter Graber's crew, and nine parachutes were observed. One crewman was killed in action (MACR #4528).

42-52078 BIG MOGUL (726th #49)
Left the USA on December 27, 1943. She was an original group aircraft flown overseas by Dale Miller's Crew #39. Condemned on July 13, 1944.

42-52079 NITEMARE (725th)
An original group aircraft, she left the USA on December 4, 1943, under the command of Richard F. Kimmel and Crew #23. Crashed at the base in Italy on May 5, 1944, during a local test flight. Her Crew Chief was George Frisbee.

42-52081 JOLLY ROGER (727th)
An original group aircraft, she departed the USA on December 10, 1943, under the command of Lewis Williams and Crew #66. Lost to fighter attacks over Ploesti on Mission #24, April 5, 1944. Lewis Williams and part of the crew were able to bail out. Four of the crew were killed (MACR #4082).

42-52078 BIG MOGUL

42-52079 NITEMARE

42-52081 THE JOLLY ROGER

42-52082 THE A-TRAIN

42-52084 MISS AMERICA

42-52082 SCREAMIN MEEMIE/THE A-TRAIN (726TH #43)
An original group aircraft, she left the USA on December 6, 1943, known as SCREAMIN MEEMIE. She was flown overseas by Crew #37, under the command of Ricarh Long. Renamed THE A-TRAIN after the popular song. She flew 59 missions, and was credited with three enemy fighters. On August 22, 1944, she returned from Mission #108 with eight major flak hits. She was deemed unfit to repair and was salvaged.

42-52084 MISS AMERICA (727th)
Departed the USA on December 10, 1943, as an original group aircraft, commanded by Paul Pfau and Crew #63. Lost to fighter attack on Mission #26 to Budapest on April 13, 1944. Paul Pfau and six of the crew were killed (MACR #4084).

42-52087 READY TEDDY

42-52094 DEVIL'S DUCHESS

42-52099 BIG IDJIT

42-52087 READY TEDDY (726th #49)

READY TEDDY was an original aircraft, leaving the USA on December 5, 1943, under the command of James L. Bell's Crew #44. Listed MIA on July 16, 1943, after Mission #83 to Wiener Neusdorf. During the flight to the target the #3 engine caught fire. READY TEDDY left the formation and spun out of control. Two of Francis Fort's crew were able to bail out (MACR #7156).

42-52092 (725th)

Departed the USA on December 2, 1943, as an original group aircraft. She was flown overseas by Crew #26 under the command of Ralph Darrow. Transferred to the 449th Bomb Group.

42-52094 DEVILS DUCHESS (725th)

An original group aircraft she departed the USA on December 2, 1943, with Crew #20 under the command of Bert G. Brown. She flew 22 known missions. Lost to fighter attack on Mission #38 to

Ploesti on May 5, 1944. Two crewmen under command of Paul Krueger were killed in action. (MACR #4604).

42-52099 BIG IDJIT (724th #30)

Departed the USA on December 2, 1943, as an original aircraft with crew #8, commanded by James Coyle. Later assigned to the 725th Bomb Squadron. Transferred to the 98th Bomb Group.

42-52101 PEACEMAKER (724th)

Departed the USA on December 4, 1943. An original group aircraft, she was flown overseas by Edward Johnson's crew. Attacked by 15 Me-109s on Mission #10 to Regensberg on February 25, 1944. Left formation at 1149 hours under fighter attack. The #3 engine caught fire. Fighter continued to attack until the plane exploded. No chutes were observed from Edward Johnson's crew. Postwar records indicate that three of the crew escaped to become POWs. (MACR #3295).

42-52102 (724th #19)

Departing the USA on December 2, 1943, she was an original aircraft flown overseas by Kent Bowlan and his Crew #17. Condemned on August 16, 1945.

42-52103 CRAVEN RAVEN (727th)

Departed the USA on December 1, 1943, as an original group aircraft under the command of Terrell Prewitt and Crew #60. Her Crew Chief was Michael Thorrick. Failed to return from Mission #24 to Ploesti on April 5, 1944. Last seen leaving the formation at the IP under fighter attack and losing altitude. Flown by Wilfred McAllister and his crew that day, five of the crew, including McAllister, perished in the aircraft (MACR # 4032).

42-52103 CRAVEN RAVEN

42-52111 OLD TAYLOR

42-52111 OLD TAYLOR (726th #44)

OLD TAYLOR had 17 airframe hours when she arrived at Fairmont AAB, Nebraska. An original aircraft, she departed the USA on December 7, 1943, with Crew #48. She was named by her original pilot, Robert Taylor. When he and his crew finished their tour OLD TAYLOR had accumulated 650 hours. She failed to return from Mission #108 to Vienna on August 22, 1944. She was hit by flak over the target and exploded, killing seven of the crew, commanded by Maurice Beaucond, Jr. (MACR #8001).

42-52114 LONESOME POLECAT (726th)

The first B-24 of Block 10 off the Ford Production line, she was an original group aircraft. Departed the USA on December 5, 1943, under command of Wilfred Bias and Crew #54. Her Crew Chief was George Hansen. On March 30, 1944, she was attacked by fighters. Cannon fire tore a huge hole in the left wing. Gunfire also killed Sgt. Andrew Wirtzberger in the nose turret. She was flown back to the base and repaired. Ditched in the Adriatic on June 10, 1944, returning from Mission #63. Two of the crew, under the command of Herbert Guiness, were lost at sea. There is no known MACR.

42-52151 OLD TUB (726th)

An original group aircraft, she departed the USA on December 7, 1943, under command of Grant Sturman with Crew #52. Crashed on take off with James Hunt and crew on February 8, 1944. Probable cause was believed to be icing. Eight of the crew were killed in the crash.

42-52153 ROMAN'S CANDLES aka
THUNDERMUG II (726th #53)

Departed the USA on December 5, 1943, as part of the original group of aircraft. Flown overseas by Frank Roman's Crew #45. Lost to flak on Mission #91 to Budapest on July 27, 1944. Flown by Harold Shauer's crew, most of the crew managed to escape, but there was one crewman listed as killed in action. (MACR #7025).

42-52114 LONESOME POLECAT

42-52153 ROMAN'S CANDLES

42-52158 BACHELOR BOMBER

42-52159 BORN TO LOSE

42-52156 SMALL FRY/LAMPLIGHTER II (726th)
An original 726th Bomb Squadron plane, she departed the USA on December 5, 1943, under the command of Charles Small and crew #42. Later transferred to the 725th Squadron. Ditched in the Adriatic on March 17, 1944, due to battle damage. Three of Ralph Darrow's crew were lost (MACR #4520).

42-52158 BACHELOR BOMBER (725th #32)
Departed the USA on December 2, 1943, as part of the group overseas movement with Crew #29, under the command of Frank Howard. Transferred on September 20, 1944.

42-52159 BORN TO LOSE (725th)
An original group aircraft, she left the USA for Italy on December 2, 1943. Flown overseas by Crew #15, under command of Verne Johnson. Transferred to the 725th Bomb Squadron, and later sent to the 449th Bomb Group. She was lost with that group on April 4, 1944.

42-52165 SLICK CHICK (725th)
Departed the USA on December 2, 1943, with Frank Hamer's Crew #32. Transferred to the 449th Bomb Group shortly after arrival in the MTO. Lost with that group on April 23, 1944.

42-52167 WEE WILLIE (725th)
Assigned to the group at Fairmont, Nebraska, she left the USA on December 2, 1943. Her original Crew #31 was under the command of Nicholas Zender. On Mission #10, February 25, 1944, she was attacked by enemy fighters at about 1140 hours. She left the formation under attack with the #2 engine on fire, which spread across the wing. Five of Richard Kimmel's crew were killed (MACR #3589).

42-52168 THE CITADEL (725th)
Departed the USA on December 5, 1943, for Italy, as an original group aircraft. She was flown overseas by Crew #35, under the command of Byron Balliet. Listed MIA on February 25, 1944, after Mission #10 to Regensburg. She was attacked by enemy fighters at about 1140 hours. Gunfire set the #3 engine on fire, and the aircraft went into a steep glide towards the ground. Nicholas Zendar and four of his crew escaped (MACR #3693).

42-52167 WEE WILLIE

42-52378 WINDY CITY #2

42-52429 BIG FAT MAMA

42-52440 CALMITY JANE

42-52460 RED RYDER

42-52246 (724th)
Left the USA on December 9, 1943. Crash landed in Turkey due to battle damage returning from Mission #27 to Bucharest, Romania, on May 15, 1944. The crew was interned, except for two that bailed out and were captured.

42-52378 WINDY CITY #2 (724th)
Departed the USA on February 2, 1944, with the 461st Bomb Group. Transferred to the 451st in May 1944. Lost to flak on July 28, 1944, with the crew of Frank Vernon, Jr. (MACR #7525).

42-52429 BIG FAT MAMA (726th #52)
Departed the USA on February 1, 1944. Failed to return from Mission #109 to Markersdorf on August 23, 1944. Attacked by fighters on the mission, and several of the engines were damaged. The crew bailed out of the stricken aircraft.

42-52440 CALAMITY JANE (725th #56 & 60)
Left the USA on February 5, 1944. Flown overseas by Frank McQuiad and crew. Damaged by flak and sent to Depot 52 on July 27, 1944, returning to the group on October 18, 1944. Listed as MIA after Mission #186 to Vienna on February 7, 1945. Paul Holst and nine of his crew were killed in action. (MACR #12091) CALAMITY JANE flew 60 known missions.

42-52449 GUMDROP (724th)
Departed the USA on February 22, 1944. Originally assigned to the 464th Bomb Group, she was transferred to the 451st in June. Later she was transferred to the 465th Bomb Group.

42-52452 STINKY POO (725th)
Transferred to the MTO from the 8th AF, she arrived on February 1, 1945. Assigned to the 451st on February 8, 1945. On February 27, 1945, she took a direct hit from flak in the #1 engine. This hit also ripped a large hole in the wing. STINKY POO left the formation. She went into a crabbed heading towards the nearest emergency airfield in Yugoslavia. She was able to make an emergency landing. The crew was returned to Bari the next day.

42-52460 RED RYDER (726th #54, #51 & #22)
Departed the USA on February 1, 1944, with the 461st Bomb Group original cadre. Transferred to the 451st on February 29, 1944. Made an emergency landing at Pascera on August 2, 1944, with major flak damage. Returned to the group on September 15. Assigned to the 725th Bomb Squadron on October 2, 1944. Later declared unfit for combat, she was returned to the USA for a Bond Tour in November 1944.

42-52501 LAKANOOKII

42-52474 (724th)
Departed the USA on March 4, 1944, arriving in April 1944. Failed to return from Mission #24 to Ploesti on April 5, 1944, with the crew of Robert L. Stone. While leading the second element the aircraft was hit by flak on the bomb run. The aircraft maintained bomb run heading while losing altitude, leading the attack unit over the target. After dropping the bombs the aircraft was attacked by fighters after the target. Eight parachutes were observed. This was the aircraft's first combat mission (MACR #3918).

42-52501 LAKANOOKIE (727th)
Departed the USA on March 27, 1944, as an original aircraft with the 484th Bomb Group. Transferred to the 451st. Lost to fighter attacks on Mission #41 to Weiner Neustadt on May 10, 1944, with the crew of Gilbert Whitfill (MACR #4838).

42-52614 LAKANOOKIE II (725th)
An original 484th aircraft she departed the USA on March 29, 1944. Transferred to the 451st in June 1944. Failed to return from Mission #94 to Bucharest on July 31, 1944, with the crew of Donald McKelvey. Damaged by flak over the target, the aircraft ran out of fuel and ditched in the Adriatic (MACR # 7209).

42-52631 (725th)
Transferred from the 8th AF on February 3, 1945, she was assigned to the 451st on March 1, 1945. She survived the war and returned to the USA on June 30, 1945.

42-52636 (727th)
Transferred from the 8th AF, she arrived in the MTO on January 9, 1945. Assigned to the 451st on January 19, 1945, to replace 42-94877 (THE JANE LEE). This aircraft crash landed on Vis on February 17, 1945.

42-64353 HOBO QUEEN (725th)
Departed the USA on March 6, 1944. Listed MIA after Mission #19 to Bolzano, Italy, on March 29, 1944, with the crew of Joseph Younger (MACR #3716).

42-64442 SUPER MOOSE (727th)
Departed the USA for Italy on December 10, 1943, as an original group aircraft. She was flown overseas by Crew #57, commanded by Roland Threadgill. Attacked by fighters on Mission #24 to Ploesti on April 5, 1944. Claremont Brownell and three other crewmen were killed in action (MACR #4081).

42-64445 PATSY JACK (727th #10)
An original group aircraft, she departed the USA on December 8, 1943, under the command of John Kavanaugh and Crew #58. PATSY JACK flew 65 known missions, and was credited with four enemy fighters. She failed to return from Mission #95 to Lepontet, France, on August 2, 1944, with George Capplelman's crew. (MACR 7208).

42-64445 PASTY JACK

42-64449 WOLF WAGON

42-64449 WOLF WAGON (724th)

Pilot John O'Conner and his crew #11 left the USA on December 2, 1944, as part of the original cadre. Returned from the April 5, 1944, mission to Ploesti with over 350 holes from flak and German fighters. John O'Conner landed her with all three tires shot out. She came to a stop in three feet of water off the landing strip at San Pancrazzio. She was deemed Class 26 and salvaged for parts.

42-64450 BODACIOUS CRITTER (727th)

An original group aircraft, she left the USA on December 10, 1943, with Earl Monniger and Crew #69. Made emergency landing at Corsica, was repaired, and returned to service on June 11, 1944. Failed to return from Mission #66 to Szony, Hungary, June 26, 1944. Lost at 1050 hours near Varazdin, Yugoslavia. THE CRITTER was attacked by five ME-109s. The entire tail section was almost shot away by cannon fire. The top turret was blown away. After a running aerial gunfight THE CRITTER went down in flames. One member of Walter Oakes, Jr.'s, crew was killed in action (MACR #6172).

42-64450 BODACIOUS CRITTER

42-64465 MAC'S FLOP HOUSE (724th)

Departed the USA on December 4, 1943, as an original aircraft of the group. Flown overseas by Roger McCollester's Crew #18. Lost to flak on Mission #41 to Weiner Neustadt on May 10, 1944, with Benjamin J. Moore and crew. (MACR #4792) This was the only known aircraft in the 451st Bomb Group to have a shark's mouth motif painted on the nose.

42-64489 MUCH WAMPUM (725TH)

An original group aircraft, she departed the USA on December 22, 1944, arriving in Italy on January 3, 1945. After a long combat career she was retired from combat and became a "hack." On February 20, 1945, she crashed into a cliff on the Island of Capri during a local taxi flight, killing nine onboard.

42-64465 MAC'S FLOP HOUSE

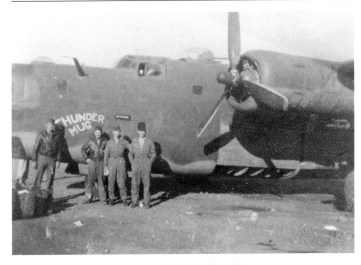

42-7475 THUNDERMUG

42-7636 THREE FEATHERS

42-7475 THUNDERMUG (726th #62)

An original group aircraft. She was flown overseas by Glen Chamber's Crew #53. Flew combat with the group until September 22, 1944, when she was transferred.

42-7636 THREE FEATHERS (726th #41)

An original group aircraft, she was flown overseas by Sidney Winski's crew. During the flight overseas the aircraft lost three engines. Pilot Sid Winski was able to make an emergency landing with three feathered props, thus the name THREE FEATHERS. Crew Chief Allan Haggerty kept her in good shape. Several crews managed to complete their combat tours in the ship. Finally deemed unfit for combat, she was salvaged on September 20, 1944. At the time of her retirement she had flown over 70 missions.

42-7687 CAVE GIRL aka THE STORK (726th #48)

An original group aircraft, she was flown overseas by Crew #46 under the command of Henry Kelly. On February 12, 1944, she suffered mechanical problems enroute. The pilot, Robert Blair, ordered the crew to bail out, and he managed to fly the aircraft back to base. She was transferred to Depot 52 on July 13, 1944.

42-7720 ST. PETER'S FERRY (727TH)

An original group aircraft that was flown overseas by William Stenning's Crew #55. Failed to return from Mission #24 to Ploesti on May 5, 1944. Was lead aircraft of the 1st attack unit when she was attacked by fighters before reaching the IP. Dropped out of formation and last seen heading towards Russian lines. Four of the crew, including William Stenning, were killed, and six became POWs (MACR #4080).

42-7687 THE STORK (CAVE GIRL)

42-7725 ADOLF AND TOJO

42-7721 LAMPLIGHTER (725th)
This original group aircraft, flown overseas by Lloyd M. Ryan and Crew #22, crash landed at Castelluccio Air Field, December 3, 1944.

42-7725 PIECEMAKER (724th)
This original aircraft was flown overseas by crew #1, under the comannd of Claude Vail. Listed as MIA on Mission #12 to Toulon, France, on March 11, 1944. ADOLF AND TOJO was hit by flak and exploded, taking Lt. Claude Vail and the entire crew to their deaths. MACR #15249 is noted for this loss.

42-7734 LAKANOOKII (725TH)
An original group aircraft flown overseas by William Tuney's Crew #19. Crash landed March 21, 1944, at Manduria due to a blown tire

during a non-operational practice flight. The aircraft was destroyed and written off.

42-7738 HARD TO GET (725th)
An original group aircraft assigned to Richard Coleman and Crew #38. Listed MIA February 10, 1944. Attacked by enemy fighters at about 1230 hours just south of the target (Regensberg). The #3 engine was observed to be smoking. The bombs were salvoed as the plane started down. It was attacked by three Me-109s. The crew managed to fly the stricken ship across the Alps to Northern Italy. It was then again attacked by fighters. Most of R.D. Coleman's crew bailed out (MACR #3284). This was the first B-24 in the group to carry the name HARD TO GET.

42-7738 HARD TO GET

42-7751 ICE COLD KATIE

42-7757 WINDY CITY

42-7751 ICE COLD KATIE (726th)
An original group aircraft that was flown overseas by Reuben Hagen's Crew #43. She blew a tire on takeoff on March 21, 1944, at San Pancrazio. Sent to Depot 52 for repair. Returned to the group on August 20, 1944. Declared Class 26 after Mission #169 to Odertal, Germany, on December 17, 1944.

42-7757 WINDY CITY (724th)
An original group aircraft flown overseas by Robert Carlson's crew #9. Lost to flak on June 6, 1944, Mission #60 to Ploesti with the crew of William Harris, Jr. (MACR #5477).

42-7759 LITTLE BUTCH (727th)
An original group aircraft flown overseas by Clarence Roach's Crew #71. Hubert Anderson was flying his first mission. Veteran Peter Massare was in the other seat on May 17, 1944. During take off the airspeed had just reached 90 mph when the left main tire blew. The aircraft skidded to a halt, and the crew escaped with two serious injuries. The aircraft did not catch fire and was salvaged for parts. At the time of the accident LITTLE BUTCH had flown 27 missions and had three fighters to her credit.

42-7763 SELDOM AVAILABLE (725th #37)
An original group aircraft, she was flown overseas by Crew #24 under command of Harold Imhoff. Failed to return from Mission #109 on August 23, 1944 (MACR #8324). Hit by flak, the crew of Willis Malakowski bailed out. SELDOM AVAILABLE crashed near Bruck.

42-7765 KNOCK-IT-OFF (724th)
An original group aircraft flown overseas by Crew #2, under the command of Nathaniel Wiersema. Listed as MIA on February 25, 1944, on Mission #10 to Regensberg. Her original pilot, Nathaniel Wiesema, and crew were attacked by fighters over Spittal, Austria, at 1200 hours. The aircraft went out of control, then leveled out. Four parachutes were observed. The fighters continued their attacks as the aircraft went out of control again and flew into a cloud bank. Post war records show that only one crewman, Sgt Alfonso Duran, was killed in action (MACR #3173).

42-7763 LITTLE BUTCH

42-7763 SELDOM AVAILABLE

42-78102 CANNON FODDER

42-78157 BODACIOUS CRITTER #2

42-78102 CANNON FODDER (726th #45)
Departed the USA on April 3, 1944. Assigned to the group in May 1944. CANNON FODDER crashed on takeoff on August 15, 1944. She flew 48 missions.

42-78145 CON JOB (727th #9)
Left the USA on April 4, 1944. Assigned to the group on May 3, 1944. Failed to return from Mission #108 to Vienna on August 22, 1944, with the crew of Richard Turnbull. Attacked by fighters, she caught fire in the waist area. The top turret gunner, John Roach, was killed (MACR #800).

42-78157 BODACIOUS CRITTER #2 (727TH)
Departed the USA on April 19, 1944. Assigned to the 451st in late May to replace 42-64450 BODACIOUS CRITTER. Her Crew Chief was T.G. Martin. On May 29, 1944, just after taking off she crashed back onto the runway and slid to a stop in a field. The entire crew managed to escape. It is believed that prop wash from the previous plane caused the accident.

42-78165 (724th)
Departed the USA on March 28, 1944, assigned to the 456th Bomb Group. Transferred to the 451st in July 1944. Damaged during a fire on the ground and salvaged on August 23, 1944.

42-78171 (725th #60)
Left the USA on April 2, 1944, assigned to the 451st in June. Sustained battle damage on June 24, 1944, and sent to 60th S.S. for repair, returning to duty on August 6, 1944. Lost to flak on Mission #109, August 23, 1944, with the crew of Glen Panyity. Four of the crew were killed (MACR #7957).

42-78145 CON JOB

42-78176 #58

42-78188 MAIRZY DOATES (SATAN'S SISTER)

42-78176 (726th #58)
Left the USA on April 20, 1944. Assigned to the group on November 24, 1944. Suffered major battle damage on January 17, 1945. Sent to depot 52 on January 18, 1945, returning on February 2, 1945. This Liberator survived combat and returned to the USA on July 26, 1945.

42-78178 (725th)
Departed the USA on March 24, 1944. Assigned to the group in June. Listed MIA after Mission #90 to Beret, Albania, on July 26, 1944, with the crew of William Schaidt. (MACR #7015)

42-78208 ESKIMO NELL

42-78188 MAIRZY DOATES aka SATAN'S SISTER (724th #31)
Departed the Zone of the Interior on March 24, 1944. This aircraft was transferred, date unknown.

42-78208 ESKIMO NELL (726th)
Departed the USA on April 16, 1944. Assigned to the group on July 18, 1944. Crashed at Vis due to battle damage returning from Mission #87 to Brut on July 22, 1944.

42-78227 MY GAL (725th #34)
Left the USA on April 28, 1944. Assigned to the group in June. Shortly after take off on August 12, 1944, a life raft came loose from the stowage compartment and was tangled in the rudder control surface. William Paddock and his copilot regained control and were able to gain enough altitude for the crew to bail out. The aircraft crashed into a field near the base.

42-78236 GAS HOUSE JR

42-78250 GOOSEY LUCY

74-78236 GAS HOUSE JR. (724th #27)

Departed the USA on April 17, 1944. Replaced the original GAS HOUSE. On Mission #93 to Budapest on July 30, 1944, GAS HOUSE JR. took a direct hit from a 88 mm shell. The shell went through the open bomb bay and through the top of the aircraft. The shell did not detonate; however, it did cause major damage to fuel lines. Paul Johnshoy and crew were able to fly the crippled Liberator back to base. Post flight inspection showed that the main spar had been damaged. GAS HOUSE JR. was repaired and returned to combat. Listed MIA after Mission #145 to Vienna on November 5, 1944, with the crew of George Heitzler (MACR #9604).

42-78250 GOOSEY LUCY (726th #50)

Left the USA on April 23, 1944. Assigned to the group on May 3, 1944. Flew her first mission on May 7, 1922. GOOSEY LUCY crashed on take off on Mission #88 to Ploesti, July 22, 1944. Five of the crew died in the crash, and five others were injured. Her crew chief was Karl Eichhorn.

42-78254 SWEATTY BETTY (727th #11)

Departed the USA on April 24, 1944. Assigned to the group in July. Made emergency landing at Vis on November 5, 1944, and returned on November 7, 1944. Crash landed at Vis on November 11, 1944, returning from Mission #148 to Aviano Airdrome, Italy.

42-78274 COCKY CREW (724TH #23)

Departed the USA on June 11, 1944. Arrived to the group in June. Reported to have been named COCKY CREW because of the crew's attitude. Made emergency landing at Vis on August 25, 1944, returning on November 11, 1944. Landed at Vis again on December 11, 1944, returning to the group on January 1, 1945. Crash landed and burned at the base after a local flight on May 7, 1945. Her Crew Chief was Philip Beckwith.

42-78254 SWEATY BETTY

42-78274 COCKY CREW

42-78276 AMERICAN MAID

42-78411 THE FLYING WOLF

42-78276 AMERICAN MAID (724th #32 & #70)
Left the USA on May 1, 1944. Assigned to the group in August 1944 to replace 42-51970. Made emergency landing at Vis on October 17, 1944, returning from Mission 3137 to Vienna. Returned to the group on November 6, 1944. She survived the war and returned to the USA on June 5, 1945.

42-78411 THE FLYING WOLF (727th #17)
Left the USA for Italy on September 20, 1944. Assigned to the group on October 16, 1944. Failed to return from Mission #173 to Oswiecim on December 26, 1944. Sustained flak damage to the #4 engine. The #1 engine was also damaged but kept running. Electrical system was also damaged. The crew of Collins Byrn was unable to transfer fuel. Just west of Lake Balaton the #3 engine ran low on fuel, and the crew began bailing out. THE FLYING WOLF crashed near Biscopce (MACR # 10750).

42-78414 BOOTS AND HIS BUDDIES

42-78436 SHADY LADY

42-78414 BOOTS AND HIS BUDDIES
aka DAM YANKEE (724th #20)
Left the USA on July 8, 1944. Listed MIA on December 2, 1944, on Mission #158 to Blechhammer. The #1 hit by flak over the target. Lost altitude and fell behind the formation. Near the Yugoslavian border the #3 engine failed and could not be feathered due to loss of oil pressure. The crew of Maurice Brown bailed out (MACR #10035).

42-78436 SHADY LADY (727th #13 & #15)
Left the USA on July 10, 1944. Originally assigned to the 461st Bomb Group. Transferred to the 451st on November 24, 1944. SHADY LADY replaced 42-95239. Failed to return from Mission #152 to Villa-Franco on December 18, 1944, with the crew of Walter Holland, Jr. (MACR #10678).

42-78445 TODDLIN TROLLOP (724th #26)
Picked up by John Winden and crew at Lincoln, Nebraska, on June 24, 1944. After modifications they departed the USA on July 5, 1944. Arriving at the 451st on July 7, 1944. The nose art was painted by crewman Frank Peterson. Lost to a direct hit from flak on Mission #108 to Vienna on August 22, 1944. Alfred M. Donnelson and his crew were killed in action. (MACR #11264)

42-78463 (725th #34)
Departed the USA on July 9, 1944. Assigned to the group on July 15, 1944. Transferred to the 484th Bomb Group on October 16, 1944, returning to the 451st on January 10, 1944. Listed MIA on Mission #187 to Vienna, February 7, 1945. After sustaining battle damage, Glenn Kerres and crew stayed with the aircraft until it ran out of fuel. They bailed out, and the plane crashed near Pettrovic (MACR #12084).

42-78445 TODDLIN' TROLLOP

42-78465 PATCHES: THE TIN TAPPERS DELIGHT

42-78471 FERTILE MYRTLE

42-78497 BUBBLE TROUBLE

42-78465 PATCHES-THE TIN TAPPERS DELIGHT (726th #53)
Departed the USA on July 10, 1944, and was assigned to the 451st in July. Sustained major flak damage on August 22, 1944. Sent to 60th S.S. for repairs, returning to service on September 5, 1944. Battle damaged again on February 14, 1945, she was repaired and returned to combat service on February 23, 1945. She was declared surplus and salvaged on August 6, 1945.

42-78471 FERTILE MYRTLE (724th #24)
Left the USA on July 8, 1944, arriving at the group on July 15, 1944. Listed MIA on Mission #109 to Markersdorf, Austria, August 23, 1944. Attacked by Fw-190s during the bomb run. Cornelious Donoghue pulled FERTILE MYRTLE away from the formation; it was last observed left wing down falling towards the ground. Seven parachutes were observed in the area. FERTILE MYRTLE crashed near Kirchberg, Austria. Cornelious Donoghue and two of the crew were killed in action (MACR #7966).

42-78523 HARD TO GET

42-78478 THE POLITICIANS (726th)
Departed the USA on July 10, 1944. This Liberator had a very short service history. She crash landed at the 451st's base on July 18, 1944, just eight days after leaving the USA.

42-78484 MERRY BARBARA (726th)
MERRY BARBARA left the USA on July 25, 1944, and was assigned to the group on August 6, 1944. Named after John W. Olds' wife. On August 17, 1944, returning from Mission #105 to Ploesti, she ran out of fuel due to flak damage and ditched in the Adriatic. Pilot John Olds survived while nine of the crew were killed. (MACR #7679) This was the sixth mission for MERRY BARBARA. Her crew chief was Karl Eichhorn. .

42-78497 BUBBLE TROUBLE (726th #41)
Departed the USA on August 4, 1944, and was originally assigned to the 461st Bomb Group. Assigned to the 451st on November 11, 1944. She survived combat and returned to the USA on June 21, 1945.

42-78523 HARD TO GET (724th #21)
Left the USA on July 22, 1944. Assigned to the 451st on August 10, 1944. She was the second Liberator to carry the name HARD TO GET in the 451st. Attacked by fighters on Mission #109 to Markersdorf, August 23, 1944. Five members of James H. Powers' crew were killed in action (MACR #7965).

42-78576 (727th)
Departed the USA on December 1, 1944. This aircraft had perhaps the shortest history with the 451st. After flying across the Atlantic she crashed during an acceptance test flight on December 5, 1944.

42-78589 (724th #21)
Left the USA on August 14, 1944, and was assigned to the group on August 27, 1944, to replace 42-78471. Received battle damage on October 21, 1944, and was sent to 60th S.S. for repair. Returned to duty and survived the war. Returned to the USA on June 5, 1945.

HARD TO GET NOSEART

42-78589 #21

42-78595 #56

42-78595 (725th #56)
Departed the USA on August 1, 1944, and assigned to the group on September 16, 1944. On October 4, 1944, the aircraft took a direct flak burst in the tail turret. The blast blew the entire turret away, killing the gunner and wounding a waist gunner. The crew made an emergency landing at Foggia Main so the wounded could get immediate medical attention. #56 was repaired and returned to service on December 23, 1944. Sustained major flak damage on January 4, 1945, sent to repair depot and returned to service on February 2, 1945. Sustained major flak damage again on February 14, 1945, and returned to service on February 21, 1945. #56 survived the war and returned to the USA on June 6, 1945.

42-78606 LEADING LADY (726th)
Left the USA on August 3, 1944, and was assigned to the 461st Bomb Group as BETTY JEAN. Transferred to the 451st on October 21, 1944, to replace 42-51483. Failed to return from Mission #173 to Oswiecim on December 26, 1944, with the crew of William F. Jackson (MACR #10785).

42-78647 (724th)
Left the USA on September 8, 1944, assigned to the group on September 23, 1944. Listed MIA on October 13, 1944, after Mission #134 to Vienna with Kenneth Elliott's crew (MACR #9048).

42-78683 (725th #47)
Left the USA for Italy on September 16, 1944, to replace 42-78595. Listed MIA a month later on October 16, 1944, after Mission #136 to Linz with the crew of Albert Johnson (MACR #9199).

42-94753 (725th)
She was known as THE PONTIAC SQUAW when she left the USA on March 29, 1944, as an original 484th Bomb Group aircraft. Transferred to the 451st. On Mission #41 to Wiener Neustadt on May 10, 1944, she was hit by "friendly fire" from a B-24. The crew of John Foster was able to fly the aircraft towards the home base. They bailed out when fuel became low. The aircraft crashed near Zagreb (MACR #4794).

42-94808 JESSE JAMES (724TH #20)
Departed the USA on April 4, 1944, and assigned to the 451st in May. Listed MIA after Mission #74 to Blechhammer on July 7, 1944, with the crew of Francis S. Russell and crew (MACR #6373).

42-94871 (724th)
This 486th Bomb Group Liberator was transferred from the 8th AF to the 451st on February 14, 1945. During ground operations on February 24, 1945, she caught fire and burned at the hard stand.

42-94877 THE JANE LEE

42-95239 APE

42-94877 THE JANE LEE (727th #6)
Left the USA on April 4, 1944, arriving to the group that month. Made a crash landing at the base on November 11, 1944, damaging the nose wheel and nose area. Sent to the 60th S.S. for repair. THE JANE LEE returned to service on January 1, 1945. The old war horse was lost due to flak on Mission #180 with the crew of Maurice Brown on January 15, 1945 (MACR #11397).

42-94908 (725th #40)
An 8th AF Liberator, she was transferred to the MTO on December 5, 1945. Assigned to the 451st on February 15, 1945. She crash landed at the base and was salvaged on March 9, 1945.

42-95236 (725th)
Ex-8th AF Liberator, she arrived in the MTO on January 10, 1944. Assigned to the 451st on February 15, 1945. Returned to the USA on June 6, 1945.

42-95239 APE (727th #4 & #75)
Left the USA for service in Italy on May 5, 1944. Assigned to the group in June 1944. Listed as MIA on Mission #144 to Kustien on November 4, 1944, with the crew William Young. The aircraft suffered mechanical problems and crashed near Chieti, Italy. Eleven crewmen were killed (MACR #9677).

42-95232 (727th)
An ex-8th AF Liberator, she arrived in the MTO on March 3, 1945, and was assigned to the group on April 7, 1945. She returned to the USA on June 12, 1945.

42-95342 (724th #29 & #31)
Left the USA on May 15, 1944, and assigned to the group in June. Lost to flak on April 25, 1945, with the crew of Frederick Ade and crew (MACR #13991).

42-95359 BABE (727th #9)
Departed the USA on May 29, 1944. Assigned to the 451st on November 24, 1944. Crash landed at Vis on December 18, 1944.

42-95342 #31

42-95359 BABE

42-95379 THE EXTRA JOKER

42-95379 EXTRA JOKER (725th #35)
Departed the USA with the crew of George Tudor. Named after an EXTRA JOKER playing card found under the plane after a poker game while enroute to the MTO. On August 23, 1944, George Tudor and crew traded aircraft with the crew of Ken Whiting. Shortly after turning at the IP the group came under fighter attack. Photographer Leo Stoustsenberger was flying in George Tudor's aircraft off the left wing of the EXTRA JOKER. One of the crew had asked him to take a photo of their EXTRA JOKER to send to the folks back home as the fighters attacked. What followed were nine of the most dramatic photos of a Liberator being shot down that would come out of the war. The EXTRA JOKER caught fire in the left wing and fell from the formation under fighter attack. After falling about 5,000 feet from the formation the aircraft exploded, killing the entire crew (MACR #7956).

42-95509 LEADING LADY (724th & 726th)
This radar Mickey Ship departed the USA on July 1, 1944, and was originally assigned to the 724th Squadron on July 13, 1944. Later assigned to the 726th, she was lost on Mission #134 to Vienna on October 13, 1944, with the crew of James Rowsey, crashing near Sankermost (MACR #9066).

42-99754 NANCY LEE (725th #59)
Departed the USA on March 9, 1944, and assigned to the group in June 1944. Listed MIA due to mechanical problems with the crew of James Evarts after Mission #74 to Bucharest, Romania, on July 3, 1944 (MACR #6378).

42-99816 WEARY WILLIE (727th #69 & 13))
Departing the USA on March 7, 1944, she was originally assigned to the 8th AF. Assigned to the group on January 3, 1945, she survived the war and returned to the USA on June 10, 1945.

44-10539 (727th)
Originally assigned to the 8th AF, arrived in Italy on December 19, 1944. Assigned to the group on January 9, 1945. Returned to the USA on June 8, 1945.

42-95509 LEADING LADY

42-99816 WEARY WILLIE

44-10539

44-10603 #49

44-10603 (726th # 49)
This was the first B-24J-70 of a block of 50 Liberators to come off the production line. She was originally assigned to the 8th AF, and arrived in Italy on December 19, 1944. She was assigned to the group on January 19, 1945. Returned to the USA on June 13, 1945.

44-10613 (726th #44)
Left the USA for service in Italy on August 24, 1944. Assigned to the group to replace 42-52111. Crash landed at Foggia Main on December 11, 1944. Returned to service on January 5, 1945. Returned to the USA on June 6, 1945.

44-10613 #44

44-10621 FUNHOUSE

44-10629 BUZZ BABY

44-10621 FULLHOUSE (724th # 25, #31 & #1)
Departed the USA on August 11, 1944, and assigned to the group that month to replace 42-78445. Made emergency landing at Vis on December 18, 1944, returning from Mission #169 to Blechhammer. The aircraft returned to service on January 18, 1945. Returned to the USA on June 5, 1944. Her Crew Chief was Philip Beckwith.

44-10629 BUZZ BABY (725th #34)
Departed the USA for Italy on August 11, 1944. Assigned to the group on September 1, 1944. Failed to return from Mission #165 to Vienna on December 11, 1944. All of the crew bailed out except for the pilot, C.R. Campbel, who was killed in the crash near Urschel (MACR # 10367).

44-10630 (726th)
Departed the USA on August 15, 1944, and was assigned to the group on August 30, 1944, to replace 42-50484. Listed MIA on November 16, 1944, with the crew of Jack Holtz. During the bomb run a bomb from a higher aircraft struck the aircraft. Two of the crew were killed in the accident. (MACR 9883).

44-10632 (725th)
Left the USA for Italy on August 8, 1944, and arrived at the group on August 11, 1944, to replace 4128816 SCRAPPY. Left the group for unknown reasons on November 11, 1944, and returned on December 16, 1944. Crash landed at Foggia Main on January 20, 1945, returning from Mission #182 to Linz, Austria.

44-40196 WEESIE (727th #16)
Departed the USA on April 23, 1944, and was assigned to the group in July 1944. On Mission #95 to LePontet Oil Storage Depot, France, WEESIE had two engines shot out by flak. Pilot Kindle young and crew were able to make it to Corsica, where the third engine was lost. They were able to make a one engine landing on that island. The plane returned to the group after repair on August 11, 1944. WEESIE failed to return from Mission #109 to Markersdorf on August 23, 1944. She was lost to flak with the crew of Robert J. Anderson, crashing near St. Aegyd (MACR # 7958).

44-40196 WEESIE

44-40438

44-41008 SLOPPY BUT SAFE

44-40418 (727th)
Transferred from the 8th AF on December 3, 1944. Assigned to the group on January 16, 1945. Sustained battle damage on Mission #186, February 7, 1945. The crew was able to fly back to Italy, and bailed out near the base after running low on fuel. The aircraft crashed and burned.

44-40421 (725th)
Transferred from the 8th AF, arriving in the MTO on December 3, 1944. Assigned to the 451st on January 13, 1945. Sustained major flak damage on Mission #182 to Linz, Austria. The aircraft was declared Class 26 and salvaged for parts.

44-40438 (727th)
Originally assigned to the 8th AF, she was transferred to the 15th AF on December 9, 1944. Arrived at the 451st on January 16, 1945. She flew 13 known missions with the 451st, and returned to the USA on June 9, 1945.

44-41008 SLOPPY BUT SAFE (727TH #7 & 13)
Departed the USA on August 9, 1944, and was assigned to the group on September 1, 1944. During an acceptance flight it was noted that the controls were rather sloppy. The controls were tightened and the aircraft was pronounced safe, thus the name SLOPPY BUT SAFE. Her nose art was painted by Gordon Snyder. She went on to fly 91 missions with the group, and returned to the USA June 6, 1945. She was later cut up for scrap. The nose art was saved and is preserved at the Commemorative Air Force Museum in Texas.

44-41056 WEESIE (42-KAY)

44-41056 WEESIE aka 42-KAY (727th #17)

Left the USA on July 21, 1944, and assigned to the group on August 6, 1944. Named after the wife of 727th Commander Kendle Young, whom he called WEESIE. Later renamed 42-KAY by new Squadron Commander John Hoppock after a combination of his pilot class and wife. 42-KAY was hit by flak several times coming off the target on Mission #134 to Vienna on October 13, 1944. The crew of Homer T. Brewer bailed out (MACR #9088).

44-41060 (725th #40)

Left the USA on July 19, 1944. Assigned to the group on August 7, 1944. Failed to return from Mission #134 to Vienna on October 13, 1944. Hit by flak after turning at the IP. One man in the nose compartment was killed by the burst. The flak also set the #3 engine on fire. The bombardier salvoed the bombs to lighten the aircraft. The aircraft lost altitude and turned towards Lake Balaton. The fire spread across the wing, and the crew of Ashley D. Smith bailed out (MACR #9051).

44-41060

44-41109 BETTY CO-ED (725th # 57 & #28)

Departed the USA on August 11, 1944. Assigned to the group on August 24, 1944. Damaged by flak and landed at Vis on December 6, 1944, returning from Mission #160 to Maribor. Returned to the group on February 4, 1945. Returned to the USA after the war on June 13, 1945.

44-4114 SASSY LASSY (725th #58)

Left the USA on July 31, 1944, with Ken Whiting's crew. They named her SASSY LASSIE, but never had the opportunity to paint the name on her. This aircraft replaced 42-78227. On Mission #109 to Markersdorf, August 23, 1944, she was flown by George Tudor's crew. Due to the difference in bombsights Tudor traded Liberators with Ken Whiting's crew. The famous photos of George Tudor's EXTRA JOKER were taken from this aircraft as fighters hammered away at the luckless EXTRA JOKER. SASSY LASIE failed to return from Mission #165 to Vienna on December 11, 1944, with the crew of Lyle Jensen (MACR #10366).

44-41109 BETTY CO-ED

44-41152 OUR GAL

44-41152 OUR GAL (727th #14)

Departed the USA on July 22, 1944. Assigned to the group on August 9, 1944, to replace 42-64445. Lost to flak with James M. Moyle's crew on Mission #143 to Vienna on October 13, 1944. One crewman was killed in action (MACR #9092).

44-41198 (726th)

Left the USA on August 4, 1945, arriving to the group on August 24, 1944. This aircraft crashed on take off on October 16, 1944, for Mission #136 to Linz, Austria.

44-41335 JEANIE (724th #28)

JEANIE left the USA for Italy on August 12, 1944. She was assigned to the group on August 27, 1944. One of her most notable missions occurred on October 13, 1944, to the Vienna area. During the bomb run the #2 engine malfunctioned. Unable to maintain formation, Pilot Thomas "Doc" Moran left the formation and joined a group of B-17s coming off the target. This group came under fighter attack, and JEANIE was hit by "friendly fire" in the wing tanks and hydraulic system. The crew nursed the plane back to the base. The crew was unable to get the main landing gear down. "Doc" brought the plane in for a nose wheel only landing at the field. The landing was perfect; none of the props were bent, and neither wing tip touched the runway. It is noted that an Army Air Force film crew was at the base and captured the landing on film. Later she made an emergency landing at Vis on December 18, 1944, returning to service on February 13, 1945. She survived the war and returned to the USA on June 10, 1945.

44-48774 (725th #56)

Departed the USA on September 17, 1944, arriving to the group on October 12, 1944. Listed MIA from Mission #186 on February 7, 1945. Hit by flak and forced out of the formation. Landed about 30 miles norhtwest of Arad at about 1600 hours. The fuel lines were repaired, and the plane was returned to the group on March 5, 1945. She survived the war and returned to the USA.

44-48774 #56

44-41335 JEANIE

44-48776 #15

44-48776 (727th #15)
Departed the USA for service in Italy on September 17, 1944. Assigned to the group on October 12, 1944. Landed at Vis due to battle damage on November 5, 1944, returning on December 3, 1944. Made emergency landing at Foggia Main on December 30, 1944, returning to the group on January 1, 1945. On Mission #190 the aircraft was hit by flak, killing copilot Walter Ross. Landed at Vis for emergency repairs. Failed to return from Mission #244 to Linz, Austria, on April 25, 1945, with the crew of Edward Stresky. Seven of the crew were killed in action. This was the second to last mission flown by the 451st. This Liberator flew 59 missions. Her Crew Chief was Albert Kvorjak.

44-48809 (727th)
Departed the USA on September 24, 1944, and assigned to the group on October 16, 1944. Made a crash landing on November 12, 1944, and sent to 60th S.S. for repair. Survived the war, returning to the USA on June 18, 1945.

44-48953 (726th #52)
Left the USA for Italy on November 29, 1944. Assigned to the group on December 15, 1944. Failed to return from Mission #211 on April 23, 1945. This aircraft later returned to the group and survived the war, returning to the USA.

44-48953 #52

44-49043 SHORT STUFF

44-49324 #40

44-49027 (727th)
Departed the USA on October 12, 1944, and was assigned to the group on November 11, 1944. She was lost on Mission #151, November 17, 1944. Hit by flak over the target, all of the crew bailed out except for the pilot, Ray Palmer, who was killed in action (MACR # 9887).

44-49043 SHORT STUFF (727th
Left the USA on December 15, 1944, and was assigned to the group on January 13, 1945. Crash landed at Zara, Yugoslavia, returning from Mission #244 on April 25, 1945.

44-49055 (726th)
This radar Mickey Ship left the USA for Italy on October 12, 1944, and was assigned to the group on November 2, 1944. Crashed into a hillside near Minervino, Italy, on January 15, 1945, during a local practice flight. Nine crew members preparing for combat were killed in this non-operation flight.

44-49218 (726th)
Departed the USA on November 18, 1944. Assigned to the group on February 1, 1945. Listed MIA on February 7, 1945, after Mission #186, with the crew of Martin Palmer. Two of the crew were killed in action (MACR #12089).

44-49324 (725th #40)
Left the USA on January 19, 1945, arriving at the group on January 29, 1945. This aircraft made an emergency landing at Foggia Main due to battle damage, returning from Mission #186 on February 7, 1945. The aircraft returned to service with the group the next day. Crashed at the 451st base on February 12, 1945.

44-49335 (724th #19)
Left the USA for Italy on February 1, 1945. Assigned to the group on February 16, 1945, to replace 42-51984 MISSFIRE II. Sustained major flak damage on Mission #203 to Augsberg, Germany, February 27, 1945. The aircraft returned to service on April 3, 1945. Returned to the USA on June 7, 1945.

44-49335 #19

44-43968 #22

44-49456 SAD SACK

44-49368 (724th #29 & #22)
This B-24L left the USA on January 31, 1945. Made an emergency landing at Zara, Yugoslavia, on February 28, 1945, and returned on April 8, 1945. Returned from Mission #218, April 22, 1945, with major flak damage. She was repaired, and returned to service on April 31, 1945. Returned to the USA on June 13, 1944.

44-49412 (724th)
Departed the USA for Italy on November 23, 1944. Assigned to the group on February 16, 1945, to replace 42-52047. Failed to return from her first combat mission on February 18, 1945. Hit by flak in the nose near Blechhammer, the nose wheel doors were blown away and left aileron control was damaged. The aircraft left the formation with the hydraulic and oxygen systems shot out. William McKinney and crew bailed out about two hours later near Deblin, Poland (MACR # 10605).

44-49414 (726th #47)
Left the USA on November 29, 1944, arriving with the group on December 19, 1944, to replace 42-51941. Listed MIA after Mission #173 to Oswiecim on December 26, 1944, with the crew of Edward Nall (MACR #10735). The aircraft was hit by flak, knocking out the two engines on the left side. The crew bailed out and evaded capture. They retured to Allied control on January 14, 1945.

44-49539 #45

44-49418 (725th)
Departed the USA on November 28, 1944. Originally assigned to the 484th Bomb Group and known as PRETTY MICKEY. Assigned to the group on December 21, 1944. Listed MIA on February 7, 1945, after Mission #186 to Vienna. Martin A. Palmer and his crew were killed in action (MACR #12059).

44-49423 (724th)
Departed the USA on October 31, 1944, for service in Italy. Assigned to the group on November 18, 1944. Lost to flak on Mission #173 to Oswiecim on December 26, 1944, with the crew of Stanley Jackson (MACR #10702).

44-49436 (725th)
Left the USA on February 1, 1945, and assigned to the group on February 15, 1945. Lost to flak on Mission #214 to Moosbierbaum with the crew of Paul Harden, April 16, 1945. The aircraft was hit in the #2 and #3 engines. Also damage to control cables. The crew was able to keep the cripple in the air until they almost reached Zara, Yugoslavia. Finally the remaining engines ran out of fuel and the crew had to bail out. (MACR #13061).

44-49437 LADY DUZZ (725th)
Left the USA on November 23, 1944. Originally assigned to the 464th Bomb Group. Transferred to the 451st on December 15, 1944, to replace 44-10629 BUZZ BABY. Believed lost to enemy action on December 26, 1944.

44-49454 SAD SACK (726th #43)
Departed the USA on December 11, 1944. Assigned to the group on January 1, 1945. Sustained major flak damage on January 31, 1945, returning to service on February 6, 1945. Suffered major flak damage on April 21, 1945. Returned to service and survived the war, returning to the USA on June 25, 1945.

44-49458 (724th #27)
Left the USA on November 29, 1944, and was assigned to the group on December 18, 1944. On Mission #210 to Vienna she was hit by "friendly fire" from another B-24. The #2 engine was hit, as well as several hits on the nose turret. The aircraft was able to make an emergency landing at Zara, Yugoslavia, where the crew made a hasty departure from the burning aircraft.

44-49460 LARRUPING LIBBY (724th)
Departed the USA for service in Italy on November 29, 1944. Assigned to the group on December 18, 1944, to replace 42-78414 BOOTS AND HIS BUDDIES. On Mission #183, January 31, 1945, the # 4 propellor ran away and could not be feathered. Unable to maintain the formation, the crew salvoed their bombs and headed toward the Russian lines. Made emergency landing about five miles south of Szolnok. The crew repaired the prop governor and flew to Vezeny, Hungary, and then to Keceskenet, Hungary. The crew left the aircraft and were taken to Bucharest, then returned to Italy March 19, 1945. (MACR #11830) .

44-49585 CHEROKEE STRIP

44-49647 #21

44-49648 #12

44-49539 (726th #45)
Departed the USA on December 3, 1944, and was assigned to the 451st on December 20, 1944, to replace 42-7751 ICE COLD KATIE. Listed MIA after Mission #208 to Bolzano on February 28, 1945. Hit by flak in the #1 engine just before the bomb release. Fell behind the formation. Near Fiume the crew had more engine trouble and took up a heading for the island of Krk. They finally had to bail out when they arrived over the island and only had one engine still running. Most of the crew returned to Italy on March 2, 1945 (MACR #12717).

44-49578 (727th)
Left the USA for Italy on December 5, 1944, and was assigned to the group on March 13, 1945. She returned to the USA on June 10, 1945.

44-49585 CHEROKEE STRIP (724h #23)
This B-24L departed the USA on December 18, 1944. Assigned to the group on February 25, 1945. She survived the war and returned to the USA on June 5, 1945.

44-49623 (726th)
Departed the USA on December 5, 1944. Originally assigned to the 461st. Transferred to the 451st on April 15, 1945. Returned to the USA on June 14, 1945.

44-49647 (724th #21)
Left the USA on December 15, 1944. Assigned to the group on January 2, 1945. Made emergency landing at Zara, Yugoslavia, on February 28, 1945, returning from Mission #175 to Venzone Railway Viaduct, Italy. Returned for repair at the 60th S.S. March 13, 1945, and then returned to Squadron service on 15 March. Returned to the USA.

44-49648 (727th #12)
Departed the USA on December 14, 1944, arriving at the group on January 3, 1945. Returned to the USA.

44-49659 THE RIP (726th)
Left the USA on December 15, 1944. Assigned to the 451st on January 5, 1945. Crash landed in Yugoslavia returning from Mission #205 to Mosbierbaum on March 1, 1945.

44-49730 (724th)
This radar Mickey Ship departed the USA for combat on December 14, 1944. She was assigned to the group on January 16, 1945. This aircraft crashed at Vis on February 13, 1945. Group records show that there was no mission on 13 February. The reason for this accident is unknown.

44-49747 WHISTLING ANNIE (724th)
Left the USA on December 14, 1944. Assigned to the group on January 3, 1945. Listed MIA on January 15, 1945, after Mission #180 to Vienna. Two members of George Bokum's crew were listed killed in action (MACR #11288).

44-49659 THE DRIP

44-49801 (724th)
Departed the USA for combat on January 19, 1945. Assigned to the group on February 2, 1945. Returned to the USA on June 14, 1945.

44-49817 (725th #33)
Left the USA on January 19, 1945. This radar Mickey Ship was assigned to the group on February 3, 1945. Returned to the USA after the war on June 8, 1945.

44-49839 (725th #59)
Left the USA for Italy on January 19, 1945. Assigned to the group on 31 January. Sustained major flak damage on Mission #192 to Neuberg Airdrome, Germany, on February 16, 1945. Declared Class 26 and salvaged on February 21, 1945.

44-49868 MALE BOX (725th # 31).
Left for combat service on January 19, 1945, and assigned to the group on January 31, 1945. Failed to return from Mission #186 on February 7, 1945. Hit by flak in the #2 engine, which caught fire. Also damaged the fuel system feeding the fire. MALE BOX exploded into three parts and fell to the ground. Albert Boyhan and three of his crew were killed in action. (MACR #12086) This was MALE BOX's third combat mission, and she had approximately 92 airframe hours.

44-49872 (726th)
This B-24L left the USA on January 19, 1945. Assigned to the group on February 3, 1945, she survived the war and returned to the USA on June 6, 1945.

44-49817 #33

44-49839 #59

44-49876 RHODA

44-49876 RHODA (726th #56)
RHODA left the USA for Italy on January 19, 1945. Assigned to the group on January 31, 1945, to replace 44-10613. Returned to the USA on June 5, 1945. Also known as THE REBEL.

44-49942 (727th)
Left the USA on January 22, 1945, assigned to the group on February 7, 1945. Returned from Mission #197 with major battle damage, and condemned on February 21, 1945.

44-50143 (726th #2)
Left the USA on January 19, 1945. Assigned to the group on February 9, 1945. This Liberator survived the war and returned to the USA on June 6, 1945.

44-50240 YE OLD FUR WAGON (727th)
This radar Mickey Ship left the USA on January 26, 1945. Assigned to the group on February 13, 1945. Returned to the USA on June 6, 1945.

44-50434 (724th)
A radar Mickey Ship, she left the USA on February 12, 1945. Assigned to the group on April 13, 1945. This Liberator survived the war and returned to the USA on June 7, 1945.

44-50443 LO-AN-ROY (727th #16 & #73)
Left the USA on February 18, 1945. Assigned to the Group on February 26, 1945. Returned to the USA on June 7, 1945.

44-50455 (725th #30)
Left the USA on February 14, 1945. Assigned to the group on 26 February. Returned to the Zone of Interior on June 29, 1945.

44-50466 (725th # 61)
This B-24M left the USA on February 14, 1945. Assigned to the group on March 7, 1945. Returned to the USA on June 12, 1945.

44-50497 (724th)
This ex-8th AF bomber was transferred to the MTO on March 6, 1945. Assigned to the group on March 15, 1945. After the war she returned to the USA on June 6, 1945.

44-50586 (726th #46)
Assigned to the group on April 5, 1945. This radar Mickey Ship survived the war and returned to the USA on June 10, 1945.

44-50591 SAKINSHACK II (724th)
Arrived at the group on February 2, 1945. Transferred to RCAF, date unknown.

44-50143 #2

44-50443 LO-ANN-ROY

44-50455 #30

44-50466 #61

44-50595 (724th)
Left the USA on February 20, 1945, and was assigned to the group on March 14, 1945. Returned to the USA on June 7, 1945.

44-50652 (725th)
Left the USA on March 1, 1945. Assigned to the group on March 6, 1945. Crashed March 27, 1945.

44-50706 (725th #38)
Left the USA on March 2, 1945, and assigned to the group on March 15, 1945. Survived the war, returning to the USA on June 6, 1945.

44-50885 (726th)
Departed the USA on March 15, 1945. Assigned to the group on April 5, 1945. Returned to the USA on June 6, 1945.

44-50905 (725th)
Left the USA for service in Italy on March 14, 1945. Assigned to the group on April 5, 1945. Transferred to the 454th Bomb Group on April 15, 1945.

44-50591 SAKINSHACK II

1

461st Bomb Group

History of the 461st Bomb Group

Under provisions of General Order Number 78, dated May 29, 1943, the 461st Bomb Group was assigned to the 2nd Air Force. The group was formally activated on July 1, 1943, at Wendover Field, Utah. Under the activation orders the group was assigned the 764th, 765th, 766th, and 767th Bomb Squadrons.

On July 29, 1943, the group was moved on paper to Gowen Field, Boise, Idaho, for assignment of personnel and equipment. The group was again transferred to Wendover on September 29, 1943, and began obtaining aircraft for training.

Colonel Fredric E. Glantzberg was given command of the group on October 24, 1943. After reviewing the facilities at Wendover, Colonel Glantzberg went to Wasington to lobby for a change of station for the group. That change came on October 28, 1943, when the group was transferred to Hammer Field, near Fresno, California.

The group completed all phases of training, and was declared ready for combat. The group echelon boarded trains for Camp Patrick Henry, Newport News, Virginia, on December 31, 1943. They departed for Italy on January 12, 1944, on four "Liberty Ships." It took over a month for the echelon to make the trip across the Atlantic, arriving on February 23, 1944.

The aircraft and crews began their departure on January 13, 1944. The route to Italy was via the southern ferry route through South America and across the Atlantic. The crossing was completed by February 24, 1944, when the last aircraft arrived at their base in Torretta, Italy.

The group flew their first mission on April 1, 1944. The results were as good as could be expected for the first mission. What else could be expected on April Fool's Day. The group would be credited with a total of 214 combat missions during their 13 months of operations in Italy.

At the close of the war the group began transferring back to the United States on July 4, 1945. After arriving in the states the group was assigned to Sioux Falls Army Air Field at Sioux Falls, South Dakota, for retraining to the B-29 Superfortress. The war in the Pacific ended before the group was ready for deployment to the Pacific.

The 461st Bomb Group was deactivated on August 27, 1945, and the personnel were seperated from the service.

The group was again activated for combat service during the Korean Conflict, and again during Vietnam.

During combat service in Italy the group had four commanding officers. Colonel Fredrick Glantzberg commanded the group from October 25, 1943, to September 22, 1944. Colonel Philip Hawes took command of the group after Col. Glantzberg completed his missions. He led the group from October 25, 1944, to Decmeber 20, 1944, when Colonel Brooks Lawhon took command.

Colonel Craven Rogers took command of the group on April 16, 1945, for the duration of the group's service in Italy.

The 461st Bomb Group was awarded two Distinguished Unit Citations. The first was awarded for the mission to the Duna Aircraft factory at Budapest, Hungary, on April 12, 1944. The second was awarded for the July 15, 1944, mission to the Credtitul Minier Oil Refinery at Ploesti, Rumania.

Markings of the 461st
When the 461st arrived in Italy, all of their B-24 aircraft wore the factory olive drab over gray paint. Except for assorted noseart that had been applied, the only other markings on the aircraft were the individual aircraft serial numbers painted on the tail.

By the time the group was assigned to the 49th Bomb Wing, the wing's new higher visibility markings were being applied. These markings consisted of the upper half of the vertical stabilizer being painted red. The 461st group identifier was a long rectangle painted on the lower half of the stabilizer. The horizontal stabilizer carried a variation of the wing marking. This was in the form of the right half being painted red, and the left side having the red rectangle painted on it.

Each aircraft was also identified by a large number painted on the front of the fuselage, and also at the rear. These numbers corresponded, for the most part, with the Squadron that the aircraft was assigned. The 764th had the low numbers, which ranged through the higher numbers assigned to the 767th Squadron.

As replacement aircraft arrived the use of noseart became more subdued. Many aircraft were never named, or if they were the noseart was not applied in the garish fashion that it had been originally. In many cases the aircraft were only adorned with the red tail marking and the aircraft in group number.

Liberators of the 461st Bomb Group

41-28670 MALFUNCTION SIRED BY FORD (766th #63)
An original group Liberator. Flown overseas by Robert Walter's crew. She was salvaged because of battle damage after Mission #10 to Belgrade, Yugoslavia, on April 17, 1944.

41-28679 HEAVEN CAN WAIT (766th #47)
Left the USA as an original group aircraft, under the command of Turner Holmes and crew. Departed the USA on January 21, 1944, Col. Frederic Glantzberg (Group Commander) flew as a passenger on this Liberator. Lost to flak on Mission #50 to Korneuberg, Austria, on June 26, 1944, with the crew of Samuel Zive (MACR #6399). This Liberator flew at least 29 missions.

41-28680 TEN ACES AND A QUEEN (766th #42)
An original group aircraft. Flown overseas by Theodore Ahlberg's crew #42. Transferred to the 47th Bomb Wing on February 28, 1944. Assigned to the 451st Bomb Group. Crashed on take off April 23, 1944, while assigned to the 451st.

41-28681 HARD GUY (765th #23)
This original group aircraft was flown overseas by Noble Taylor and crew. Crashed on December 2, 1944.

41-28683 ZOMBIE OF 69 (767th #69)
An original group aircraft. Flown overseas by William Wright's crew. She crashed during a training mission while the group was still in North Africa.

41-28679 HEAVEN CAN WAIT

44-50706 #38 (SEE T.S. THE CHAPLIN)

41-28681 HARD GUY

41-28685 LEADING LADY

41-28693 WAR EAGLE

41-28685 LEADING LADY (765th #24)
An original group Liberator, she was flown overseas by Marion Mixson's crew. Lost to flak on MIssion #36 to Ploesti on May 31, 1944, with the crew of Samuel Norris (MACR #6126). The pilot, Samuel Norris, was the only member of the crew killed.

41-28689 SWEET CHARIOT (766TH)
Left the USA as part of the original group cadre. Failed to return from Mission #88 to St. Polten, Austria, on August 23, 1944, with the crew of Gordon Rosencrans, Jr. (MACR #8766).

41-28693 WAR EAGLE (764th #1)
An original group aircraft. Flown overseas by Clyde Stevens' crew. Lost to flak with the crew of Richard Freeman on Mission #69 to Linz, Austria, on July 25, 1944 (MACR #11977). Her Crew Chief was Richard Eley

41-28708 THE MOUNTAINEER (766th #55)
This Liberator departed the USA as part of the original cadre. Flown overseas by Curlos Settle's crew #55. One of 10 aircraft transferred to the 47th Bomb Wing on February 28, 1944. She was condemned on August 16, 1944.

41-28717 BIG STINKY (765th #30)
An original group aircraft. Flown overseas by Crew #30, commanded by Forrest Nixon. Lost to flak on Mission #14 to Bucharest on April 24, 1944, with the crew of Forrest Nixon, Jr. (MACR #4627). BIG STINKY took a direct flak burst in the bomb bay area and caught fire. Forrest Nixon pulled away from the formation just before the Liberator exploded.

41-28717 BIG STINKY

41-28725 INVICTUS

41-28726 MISTER PERIOD (.)

41-28724 JIZZY OUTCH (767TH #71)
Left the USA under the command of William Wright and crew as part of the original cadre. Crashed returning from Mission #13 on April 23, 1944.

41-28725 INVICTUS (765th #27 & #21)
An original group aircraft. Flown overseas by the crew of Thomas Moss. The artwork was painted on the nose of the Liberator before leaving the states. Salvaged on August 4, 1944. It is noted in the Official Group History that she returned from the repair depot and was used for non-combat flights.

41-28726 MISTER . (PERIOD) (764th #6)
This original group aircraft was given her name when the pilot was informed that he was going to become a father just before leaving for Italy. She crash landed and was written off after Mission #43 to Porto Marghera, Italy, on June 10, 1944.

41-28732 SWEE' PEA (764th #18)
An original group aircraft, flown overseas by the crew of Edgar Trenner. Damaged by enemy action on Mission #69 to Linz, Austria, on July 25, 1944. The crew was able to fly back to Italy. They used parachutes to try and slow the airspeed down after landing. Unable to stop, the aircraft ran off the runway and was destroyed. The crew was able to walk away from the wreckage.

41-28734 NOV SHMOZ KA POP ? (764th #15)
An original group Liberator flown overseas by Crew 15 and commanded by John Wilson. On Mission #80 to Genoa, Italy, she was flown by F/O James Cain's crew. Over the target a fire developed from what is believed to be flak damage. Without warning the aircraft exploded. Two men were observed bailing out of the wreckage, however, none of the crew survived. Several of the aircraft in the formation returned to Torretta with pieces of the aircraft imbedded in them. It is interesting to note that the MACR #16376 was not written until April 10, 1945.

41-28732 SWEE' PEA

41-28734 NOV SHMOZ KA POP ?

41-28737 RHODE ISLAND RED

41-28903 MYRA G

41-28737 RHODE ISLAND RED (765th #20)
RHODE ISLAND RED was an original group Liberator flown to Italy by Samuel Norris and crew. Crew Chief was Robert Basiliere. She was salvaged due to battle damage after Mission #83 to Frejus, France, on August 15, 1944.

41-28740 THE BAT (765th #36)
Departed the USA on February 1, 1944, as an original Liberator commanded by Jackson Childrey. Transferred to the 451st Bomb Group on February 28, 1944. Renamed RHODA, she was lost on April 24, 1944.

41-28836 (767th #61)
Departed the USA on April 24, 1944. Originally assigned to the 484th Bomb Group. Attacked by fighters on Mission #69 to Linz, Austria, on July 25, 1944. Lost with the crew of Robert Fisher (MACR #7038).

41-28850 (766th #44)
Departed the USA on April 16, 1944. Lost to fighter attacks on Mission #69 to Linz, Austria, on July 25, 1944, with the crew of Joseph Hesser (MACR #1000).

41-28856 (764th #7) LADY DUZZ
Departed the USA on May 29, 1944. Condemned on 12-18-44 after the mission to Blechhammer.

41-28858 LADY EDITH (765th #28)
Departed the USA on May 20, 1944. Condemned on April 14, 1945.

41-28861 (767th #74)
Transferred from the 451st on July 29, 1944, this radar Mickey Ship served with the 461st for a very short time. She was again transferred back to the 451st. She completed the war and returned to the USA. She was originally named BURMA BOUND, and was later called LITTLE BOY TOO.

41-28867 SLEEPY TIME GAL (765th #21)
Departed the USA on April 2, 1944. Attacked by fighters on Mission #69 to Linz, Austria, on July 25, 1944. Lost with the crew of Kenneth Githers (MACR #7113).

41-28740 THE BAT

41-28970 LIBERTY BELLE

41-28903 MYRA G (764th #18)
Departed the USA on June 6, 1944. This radar Mickey Ship was originally assigned to the 451st Bomb Group. Transferred to the 461st in late June 1944. Her Crew Chief was Henry Jones. She was named after his newly born daughter. On April 16, 1945, she received a direct burst of flak in the radio room area. She managed to make it back to Torretta, where she was declared Class 26.

41-28913 (765th & 767th #36 & 67)
Left the USA for Italy on April 20, 1944. Lost on December 17, 1944, on Mission #151. Originally assigned to the 765th, she was later assigned to the 767th Squadron. Robert Galvan's #67 was flying in the #2 position of the lead flight when attacked by Fw-190s. The #3 engine was hit and burst in flames. The crew was able to crash land the damaged aircraft near Roznava, Slovakia, and survived.

41-29284 PLASTERED BASTARD

41-28940 (765th #36)
Departed the USA on April 20, 1944. Crashed November 12, 1944, during a test flight.

41-29870 LIBERTY BELLE (765th #33)
Departed the USA on April 17, 1944. Lost on Mission #75, August 3, 1944. The crew of Robert Schweisberger's crew failed to return due to mechanical problems (MACR #7199). She was last seen just south of the Alps with the #3 supercharger on fire. They were able to crash land on a beach in Northern Italy, and several of the crew returned on October 3, 1944.

41-29006 (766th)
Departed the USA on April 17, 1944. Lost on Mission #138 to Blechhammer on November 20, 1944. Damaged by flak over the target, the Liberator ditched in the Adriatic near the Italian coast when it ran out of fuel. Charles Krahn and four crewmen were lost at sea. There is no known MACR for this incident.

41-29268 TOU JOUR GAY. (766TH #52)
An original group aircraft. Salvaged on June 22, 1944

41-29284 THE PLASTERED BASTARD (765th #28)
Delivered to the group on January 6, 1944. Assigned to Crew #28, commanded by Vernon Garrison. Departed the USA on February 12, 1944. Arrived at Torretta Field, Italy, on March 8, 1944. It was the last aircraft to arrive in Italy. On May 10, 1944, she had two engines shot out and made an emergency landing. Returned to service, but she was badly damaged when a landing gear collapsed after a test flight on August 4, 1944. Believed to have been sent to Depot 52, and was salvaged on July 19, 1945.

41-29289 BATTLE CRATE (764th #5)
BATTLE CRATE was an original group aircraft flown overseas by Crew 5, commanded by Keith Fuller. Crashed due to mechanical problems returning from Mission #54 to Bucharest. Her crew on that day was under the command of Mac Lucus (MACR #6377). The crew bailed out near the Yugoslavian coast.

41-29289 BATTLE CRATE

41-29313 HOTTEST ??? IN TOWN

41-29313 HOTTEST ??? IN TOWN (766th #45)
Her nose art was painted by Assistant Crew Chief Ted Wise before the ship left for Italy as part of the original cadre. Her original name was HOTTEST ASS IN TOWN, but the base commander did not like the name, so question marks were used to censor the word ASS. She was flown overseas by Joseph Donovan, who led the first

flight on the overseas movement. On Mission #67 to Ploesti on July 22, 1944, she was badly damaged by enemy action. The crew of Turner Holmes was able to limp back to Italy. Unable to lower the landing gear, Holmes had the crew bail out over Torretta. After heading the plane towards the Adriatic he also bailed out. THE HOTTEST ??? IN TOWN crashed near the Canosa Road.

41-29321 (767th #64)
An original group aircraft, flown overseas by Harold Strong's crew. She survived the war and returned to the USA on June 8, 1945.

41-29325 HARE POWER (765th #29)
Departed the USA on February 2, 1944, as part of the original group under command of Eugene Ford. Transferred to the 460th Bomb Group on February 28, 1944. Later transferred to the 454th Bomb Group. She completed the war and returned to the USA on June 27, 1945.

41-29332 (767th #67)
Departed the USA on January 27, 1944, as an original group aircraft under command of Ausbon Aldredge. One of 10 aircraft to be transferred to the 47th Bomb Wing on arrival. This aircraft was assigned to the 450th Bomb Group, where she was called BOOBIE TRAP. Ultimately salvaged on April 17, 1945.

41-29325 HARE POWER

41-29332 BOOBIE TRAP

41-29333 STINKY

41-29333 STINKY (764th #3)
An original group aircraft, she was flown overseas by the crew of James Bean. Her Crew Chief was Alan Bro. Salvaged due to battle damage on November 5, 1944. It is believed that she may have been stripped of armament and used as a squadron "hack."

41-29334 OL' BIRD (764th #11)
An original group aircraft. Survived the war, and was salvaged on June 20, 1945.

41-29335 EVIL WEEVIL (764th #9)
This was an original group Liberator. She was flown overseas by Robert Hefling's crew. Her crew chief was Henry Jones. She was salvaged on February 11, 1945.

41-29336 HI HO SILVER (766th #50)
An original group aircraft. Lost on the first group mission April 4, 1944. Flown by Sidney Wilson's crew, they were involved in a mid-air collision with 42-52388 (OUR BABY). Two of the crew were killed (MACR #4087).

41-29337 DWATTED WABBIT (766th #53)
Departed the USA as part of the original group cadre under command of William Banes, Jr. Damaged by flak on Mission #60 to Nimes, France. The crew of William Barnes, Jr., ditched in the Mediterranean Sea near Toulon, France, trying to return. (MACR #6808)

41-29334 OL' BIRD

41-29335 EVIL WEEVIL

41-29337 DWATTED RABBIT

41-29362 LUCKY SEVEN

41-29338 SCROUNCH (764th #10)
Departed the USA on February 7, 1944, as part of the original cadre. One of 10 Liberators transferred to the 47th Wing on arrival. This Liberator was transferred to the 450th Bomb Group and renamed MARY JANE. She was lost with that group on April 25, 1944.

41-29241 (767th #76) WHEELS OF JUSTICE
An original group Liberator, flown overseas by George Nelson's crew. She crashed on April 20, 1944.

41-29362 LUCKY SEVEN (764th #7)
An original group Liberator, she departed the USA on 10 February, arriving overseas on February 25, 1944. On Mission #67 to Ploesti on July 22, 1944, she was flown by the crew of Clarence Bloxam. Shortly after crossing the Adriatic the #2 engine was lost and the prop feathered. Near the target flak knocked out another engine and the electrical system. Five of the crew bailed out. Five of the crew rode LUCKY SEVEN down, and made a crash landing in a wheat field near Alexandria. The navigator was killed when his parachute failed. The rest of the crew were made POWs in Bucharest.

41-29367 (765th #32)
An original group aircraft, she was flown overseas by Crew #32, commanded by Joseph Sage. Caught fire at about 0445 hrs on May 5, 1944, during servicing for the mission. Exploded when over 900 pounds of bombs went off. Parts of the aircraft were found near the control tower, and for over a quarter of a mile.

41-29517 PISCES (766th #51)
Originally assigned to the 8th AF "Zodiacs." Condemned on June 19, 1945.

41-29519
Departed the USA on March 27, 1944, as an original Liberator of the 484th Bomb Group. Salvaged on June 9, 1945.

41-29529 (765th #23)
Departed the USA on March 27, 1944. Assigned to the 484th, this ship was transferred to the 461st. Listed MIA with the crew of Robert Warren, Jr., on July 25, 1944 (MACR #9844).

41-29517 PISCES

42-50303 OUR HOBBY

41-29870 LIBERTY BELLE (765 #33)
Departed the USA for Italy on April 17, 1944. Failed to return from Mission #75 on August #, 1944. The crew of Robert Schweisberger was lost to mechanical problems (MACR #7199).

42-50303 OUR HOBBY (765th #20 1/2)
Departed the USA on April 30, 1944. Lost to flak on Mission #62 to Ploesti on July 15, 1944, with the crew of William Weems, Jr. (MACR #6962).

42-50397 (765th #36)
Departed the USA on May 15, 1944, after modification to a radar Mickey Ship. On July 22, 1944, this Liberator was flown by several crewmen who were near their magic "fifty." Col. Glantzberg was also aboard, and would lead the mission. After turning at the IP the aircraft was hit in the #4 engine and fuel tank, which burst into flame. The #3 engine also quit. The ship fell from the formation out of control. The flight deck crew rang the bail out bell. During the dive the fire went out, and the crew was able to recover the aircraft. The engineer was able to plug a fuel line with a .50 caliber shell and transfer fuel. The crew threw everything out that they could, and managed to bring the ship back to Torretta. The brand new Mickey Ship was declared Class 26 after her first mission.

42-50605 LO AND BEHOLD (766th)
Departed the USA for Italy on July 8, 1944. Returned to the USA after the war.

42-50613 HOLY JOE (764th)
Departed the USA on January 7, 1945, and was assigned to the 8th AF. Later transferred to the MTO. Survived the war and returned to the USA.

42-50948 (766th #26)
Failed to return from Mission #67 to Ploesti on July 22, 1944, with the crew of Elias Moses (MACR #7005).

42-50953 THE FLYING FINGER (765th)
Left the USA for Italy on July 14, 1944. Attacked by fighters on Mission #151 to Odertal, Germany, on December 17, 1944. Gunfire hit the #3 engine, which Pilot Philip Crossman feathered. Gunfire also hit the nose and the #4 engine. Four of the crew were killed in action. This was the crew's 10th mission (MACR #10677).

42-50970 LAZY LADY (764th #12)
Departed the USA on August 3, 1944. Originally assigned to the 484th Bomb Group. Listed MIA after Mission #108 to Munich on October 4, 1944. Lost to flak with the crew of John Turner, Jr. (MACR #8975).

42-50970 LAZY LADY

42-51319 ZOMBIE OF 69

42-51378 (765th #25)
Lost to flak on Mission #164 to Linz on January 20, 1945. Flown by the crew of James Yancy, the aircraft was seen to explode over the target (MACR #11806).

42-51319 (767th #69) WELCOME WAGON
Departed for service in Italy on July 18, 1944. Lost to fighter attack on Mission #151 on December 17, 1944. She was flown that day by a crew commanded by Fredrick Capalbo. Attacked by fighters before the IP. The #3 engine was shot out. The Liberator left the formation and was on fire in the bomb bay. Three of the crew were killed when the B-24 exploded (MACR #10651).

42-51322 (767th #66)
Departed for Italy on July 20, 1944. MIA on December 17, 1944. On Mission #151 she was flown by the crew of Charles Lang, Jr. The Liberator was attacked by Fw-190s. The #3 engine was hit, and the aircraft left formation under fighter attack. Unable to stay in the air, the crew bailed out as the aircraft exploded. Seven of the crew were captured. Three evaded and were returned to the 15th Air Force (MACR #10742).

42-51324 TEN MEN BAK aka PAULETTE (765th #12)
Left the USA for Italy on July 25, 1944. Failed to return from Mission #151 on December 17, 1944. The crew encountered problems when the #3 supercharger failed near Bratislavia, Czechoslovakia. The #2 engine also started to run rough. Unable to maintain formation, the crew took up a heading for the Russian lines. The aircraft was damaged by flak, and it was then attacked by fighters. Gunfire from the fighters killed two of the crew. The Liberator caught fire, and the remaining crew began to bail out. As the aircraft fell, she came apart from the force of the dive. Other members of Gerald Smith's crew survived. The aircraft crashed near Omsenie, Czechoslovakia (MACR #10683).

42-51336 SHADY LADY (766th)
Departed the USA on July 20, 1944. Lost to fighter attack on Mission #89, August 24, 1944. The crew for this day's mission was commanded by John Wren, Jr. (MACR #8327) The crew bailed out North of Rimini, Italy

42-51338 (766th)
Departed the USA on August 15, 1944. Lost to flak on Mission #108 to Munich on October 4, 1944, with the crew of Robert Falkner (MACR #8932).

42-51346 JAKE'S NEIGHBOR (765th #31)
Left for service in Italy on July 31, 1944. Lost with the crew of Clarence Marshall on Mission #150 to Brux on December 15, 1944 (MACR #10676).

42-51378 (765th #25)
Departed for service in Italy on August 27, 1944. Lost to flak on Mission #64 to Linz, Austria, with the crew of James Yancey (MACR #11806).

42-51406 (764th #11)
Departed the USA on September 4, 1944. She was flown overseas to Italy by William Guyton. They called the plane SURREY WITH THE FRINGE ON TOP. They went to another Squadron. There is no record of that name being painted on the Liberator. Crashed on February 7, 1945.

42-51422 (767th #72)
Departed the USA on September 8, 1944. Crashed November 20, 1944.

42-51430 THE TULSAMERICAN (765th #24)
This was the last Liberator to come off the assembly line at Tulsa, Oklahoma, and purchased by workers using war bonds, thus the name. Departed the USA on September 17, 1944, under the command of William Donalds. Assigned to the 461st in October 1944. Crashed December 17, 1944.

42-51422 #72

42-51430 TULSAMERICAN

42-51474 THUNDERMUG (765th #63)
Departed the USA on July 25, 1944. The nose art of a baby with lightning in one hand and a bomb in the other, sitting on a potty was painted by Wayne Pifer. Survived the war and returned to the USA on June 12, 1945.

42-51501 ZOMBIE OF 69 II (767th #69)
Departed the USA on December 19, 1944, and assigned to the 8th AF. Transferred to the MTO, the aircraft was assigned to the 461st and named ZOMBIE OF 69 II in honor of the first ZOMBIE OF 69. Her Crew Chief was Seth McKinney. Salvaged due to battle damage after Mission #195 on March 14, 1945.

42-51599 PIECEMAKER (765TH #34)
Departed the USA on December 19, 1944, and assigned to the 8th AF. Later transferred to the 15th AF. Returned to the USA.

42-51606 IGGY (764th #9)
Departed the USA on August 3, 1944. This was the Liberator used by Col. Glantzberg for his farewell flight on September 22, 1944. Returned from Mission #111 to Komaron, Hungary, on October 7, 1944, with severe battle damage. Declared Class 26, and salvaged on October 8, 1944.

42-51610 MAJORIE H (765th)
Left the USA for Italy on September 23, 1944. Lost to flak with the crew of Lawrence Woodruff on Mission #181 to Vienna on February 21, 1945. (MACR #12473) The crew returned to the group on March 36, 1945.

42-51501 ZOMBIE OF 69

42-51606 IGGY

42-51783 WHAT'S NEXT !

42 51695 (765th #39)

Departed the USA on September 8, 1944. On February 11, 1945, she returned with extensive damage to the hydraulic system. Pilot Robert Kelliher circled the base for over two hours while the crew tried to hand crank the landing gear down and get it locked. Running low on fuel, he ordered most of the crew to bail out over the base. He and two other crewmen managed to make a crash landing after dark. The aircraft was written off.

42-51759 (766th)

Left for service in Italy on September 6, 1944. Survived the war and returned to the Zone of Interior on June 11, 1945.

42-51778 HI-HO SILVER (765th #23)

Departed the USA on August 17, 1944. Transferred to the 2641st, 885 BS (Carpetbaggers). Listed MIA with that group on October 16, 1944 (MACR 9679).

42-51783 WHAT'S NEXT ! ? (765th #35)

Departed the USA on August 21, 1944. This particular B-24 had a reputation of being a "problem ship." It always seemed that something went wrong, hence the name WHAT'S NEXT !?. Hit by flak over Linz, Austria, on Mission #204, March 25, 1945. Sustained major damage to the left wing near the wheel well. The crew of Edward Demmond was able to fly back to Torretta. On approach they were informed by the tower that the left gear had fallen off. Seven of the crew bailed out over the field. The pilot then bellied the ship in with the rest of the crew onboard. The Liberator was written off and salvaged.

42-51816 EVIL WEEVIL TOO (764th)

Departed the USA on August 28, 1844. Transferred to the 484th, and then to another group. Crashed on June 4, 1945.

42-51838 (766th #65)

Departed for Italy on August 26, 1944. Crashed during a POW supply flight after the war on May 31, 1945. Left formation enroute with the crew of Cleone Conner, Jr. (MACR #13485).

42-51838 #65

42-51925 EL PAGLIACCIO

42-51922 (765th)
Left for Italy on August 21, 1944. Listed as MIA on December 16, 1944, with the crew of Lee Ward. (MACR #10494) It is interesting to note that the 461st did not fly a mission on this day. It is possible that the aircraft was actually lost on 15 December.

42-51925 PAGLIACCIO (764th #14)
Departed the USA on August 21, 1944, and assigned to the 484th Bomb Group. Transferred to the 461st.

42-51937 (764th)
Departed the USA on September 16, 1944. Returned to the Zone of Interior on July 24, 1945.

42-51946 (764th #1)
Departed for service in Italy on December 9, 1944. Returned after the war on June 8, 1945.

42-51949 (766th)
Left the Zone of Interior on August 27, 1944. Returned after the war on June 14, 1945.

42-51967 STRANGE CARGO (765th #34)
Departed the USA on September 2, 1944, and assigned to the 484th Bomb Group, where she was called STRANGE CARGO. Transferred to the 461st.

42-51971 (765th)
Left for service in Italy on October 5, 1944. A radar Mickey Ship, she was lost due to weather problems (believed icing) on Mission #132 to Innsbruck on November 15, 1944. William Beatty and seven of the crew were killed (MACR #9885).

42-51867 (765th)
Departed for Italy on August 27, 1944. Returned to the USA on June 9, 1945.

42-51898 (767th)
Departed the Zone of Interior on August 26, 1944. Lost to flak with the crew of Edward George on Mission #152 to Blechhammer on December 18, 1944 (MACR #10639).

42-51918 (766th)
Departed the USA on September 17, 1944. Damaged by flak over Stasshof on Mission #205. The crew of Randell Web was able to crash land at Pecs, Hungary (MACR #13198).

42-51967 STRANGE CARGO

42 52025 ARSENIC AND LACE

42-52025 ARSENIC AND LACE (765th #26)

Departed the USA for Italy on September 22, 1944. The crew of Gerald Smith was flying their 12th mission on December 17, 1944. ARSENIC AND LACE was attacked by fighters about nine minutes from the target, knocking out the #3 engine. Gunfire killed gunners Edwin Howard and Abraham Abramson in the waist. The aircraft slid from the formation, and shortly after leaving the formation the wing collapsed and the fuel tank exploded. Five of the crew rode the plane to the ground (MACR #10680).

42-52052 (765th) ALMA-M-AMUR #27

Left for Italy on December 15, 1944. Returned after the war on July 2, 1945.

42-52053 (766th)

Departed the USA on January 3, 1945. Transferred to the 454th Bomb Group.

42-52065 (766th) HOME TOWN GAL #63

Departed the USA on October 5, 1944. Returned to USA on June 8, 1945.

42-52325 BUSHWACKER (767TH #60)

This original group Liberator was flown overseas by Floyd Woodward's crew. Her Crew Chief was Odess Lovin. Crash landed returning from Mission #132 on November 15, 1944. This was her 45th mission. The name BUSHWACKER was painted on the aircraft by Wayne Pifer about half an hour before she took off on her last mission, November 15, 1944.

42-52336 (766th #49)

An original group Liberator, she was flown overseas by the crew of Paul Mowery. Mowery and his copilot were killed due to a mid-air collision on April 13, 1944, during Mission #7 to Budapest. The other aircraft (42-52366) had been hit by flak and fell into this Liberator (MACR #4649).

42-52361 (765th #22)

Flown overseas by John Specht's crew as part of the original cadre. Returning from Mission #4 to Zagreb on April 6, 1944, the crew jettisoned the fragmentation bombs over the Adriatic. One of the bombs detonated, causing fires in the bomb bay and waist area. Two of the crew bailed out in the area of Vis. Flight Engineer E.D. McGaugh managed to put the fires out and repair the broken fuel line. The pilot was able to fly the crippled Liberator to Italy, where the rest of the crew bailed out near Foggia. For their action that day John Specht (pilot), Robert Appplegate (copilot), and Everett McGaugh (flight Engineer) were awarded the Distinguished Flying Cross.

42-52366 SPIRIT OF HOLLYWOOD /GLORIA JEAN (766th #44)

An original Liberator, she was flown overseas by Charles Bauman's crew #44. On Mission #7 to Budapest, April 13, 1944, she was lost to flak with this crew. On that mission they were flying deputy lead position in A flight in the second section. The flak burst blew a large portion of the wing off. The Liberator went out of control and fell into the aircraft in the number four slot, which was flown by Paul Mowery's crew (42-52336) (MACR #3974).

42-52368 PIECEMAKER (765TH #34)

An original group aircraft, she was flown overseas by the crew of William Weems. Returned from Mission #4 on April 6, 1944, with hydraulics shot out. William Weems ran the Liberator off the strip to stop. Repaired and returned to service. Lost to fighter attack on Mission #69 to Linz on July 25, 1944, with Glennial Fulks' crew (MACR #7110).

42-52371 UPSTAIRS MAID (765th #37)

This original group Liberator was flown overseas by Crew #37, commanded by Roy Huber. She was badly damaged by flak and fighters on July 25, 1944, and sent to the repair depot. Returned to service in October 1944. UPSTAIRS MAID survived the war, and returned to the USA on June 27, 1945.

42-52368 PEACEMAKER

42-52371 UPSTAIRS MAID

42-52378 OMAHA ANN (767th #74)
An original group Liberator. She was given her name as a joke when one of her crew received a "Dear John" letter meant for someone else. The name was applied with chalk. Transferred to the 451st Bomb Group on February 28, 1944, where she was named WINDY CITY II. Lost with the 451st on July 28, 1944.

42-52379 (765th #4)
An original group Liberator, she was flown overseas by the crew of Mac Kollenborn. While taxiing after a training flight at Oudna, the copilot accidentally retracted the landing gear; this caused the Liberator to be damaged beyond repair.

42-52388 OUR BABY (767TH #62)
Flown overseas by the crew of William Zumsteg as part of the original cadre. Lost on April 2, 1944, with this crew on the group's first operational mission. Collided with HI HO SILVER near Bihac, Yugoslavia (MACR #4086). Several of the crew were able to bail out after the accident.

42-52389 JUG BUTT (766th #58)
An original group aircraft, she departed the USA on January 21, 1944. Flown overseas by Joseph Hesser and crew #56. Believed condemned after training mishap on April 27, 1944.

42-52393 ONE EYED JACK (764th #2)
An original group aircraft flown overseas by Harold Blanchard and crew; they departed the USA on February 1, 1944, arriving on 4 February. Her Crew Chief was John Gatz. This Liberator presents a historical dilemma. According to the Individual Aircraft Card she crashed on February 29, 1944. She also shows up on the 98th Bomb Group records. Photos of the aircraft indicate that she flew 29 missions. Listed on an individual combat record as having flown missions as late as July 16, 1944.

42-52378 OMAHA ANN

42-52388 OUR BABY

42-52389 JUG-BUTT

42-52393 ONE EYED JACK

42-52395 LITTLE JESUS (767th #60)
An original group aircraft flown overseas by Floyd Woodard's Crew #60. Lost to flak with that crew on Mission #9 to Belgrade on April 16, 1944. (MACR #4022).

42-52396 FLAK FINDER (767th #73)
Flown overseas by Francis Riley and crew as an original group aircraft, departing the USA on January 27, 1944. One of 10 aircraft transferred to the 47th Wing on arrival. FLAK FINDER was assigned to the 449th Bomb Group on March 3, 1944. Renamed SUSAN JANE, she was lost with that group on May 29, 1944.

42-52398 BOISE BELLE (766th #41)
An original group aircraft, flown overseas by Donald MacDonald's crew. Salvaged due to battle damage on April 24, 1945, after Mission #227.

42-52398 BOISE BELLE

42-52399 MISS CARRIAGE

42-52408 THE KISSED OFF KIDS

42-52399 MISS CARRIAGE (767th #73)
Left the USA on January 27, 1944, as part of the original cadre under the command of Gerald Maroney. On Mission #30, on May 24, 1944, she was hit by flak. Due to the damage, Gerald Moroney and crew headed towards Switzerland. Unable to make it, they bailed out over France. MISS CARRIAGE crashed near the summit of Pic de I'Aiglo, a mountain near Thorenc, France. Four of the crew were captured. Six of the crew evaded capture until returning to Allied control in September 1944 (MACR #5416).

42-52405 (766th #54)
Flown overseas by the crew of Robert Bigelow's crew as part of the original cadre. Lost to flak on Mission #30, May 24, 1944, with the crew commanded by Robert Bigelow. Four of the crew were killed in action (MACR #5041).

42-52407 (767th #67)
An original group Liberator, she was flown overseas by James Harris and Crew #65. After a long combat career, she was salvaged due to battle damage on March 2, 1945.

42-52408 THE KISSED OFF KIDS (766th #43)
Flown overseas by Ralph Seeman's crew as an original group aircraft. Badly damaged after belly landing returning from a practice mission on August 24, 1944. At this point she had flown 50 missions. Repaired and returned to service. Listed MIA on Mission #181 on February 21, 1945 (MACR #12359).

42-52409 HELL'S A POPIN (764th #16)
An original group Liberator, she was flown by Kay Steele's crew. Lost with that crew on April 13, 1944, on Mission #7 to Budapest, Hungary (MACR #3973).

42-52412 THE PURPLE SHAFT (767th #75)
An original group Liberator believed to have been flown overseas by Harry Huggard's crew. Returned to the USA on June 9, 1945.

42-52418 Mary L (765th #33)
An original group Liberator. On May 6, 1944, 41-29367 caught fire and exploded. An engine from that aircraft landed on this aircraft and caused severe damage. Due to this damage the Liberator was declared Class 26 on May 8, 1944.

42-52436 DOWN 'N GO (766th #48)
An original group Liberator, she was flown overseas by the crew commanded by Douglas Robertson. Lost due to mechanical problems on Mission #77, August 7, 1944, with the crew of Robert Sterrett (MACR #11267). Last seen leaving the formation with two engines out.

42-52412 THE PURPLE SHAFT

42-52436 DOWN 'N GO

42-52458 CHIPPIEDALL

42-52451 (767th #66)

An original group aircraft. Lost to fighter attacks on Mission #69 with the crew of John Kane (MACR #7004).

42-52458 CHIPPIEDAL (764th #13)

Assigned to the group as an original aircraft with less than 25 hours on her airframe. James Hardy was assigned as her crew chief. Flown overseas by Robert Sayre's crew. She flew the group's first 31 missions without an abort. She was lost on June 11, 1944, with Robert Hefling's crew (MACR #6307). This was CHIPPIEDAL's 37th mission.

42-52459 WINONA BELLE (764th #8)

An original group aircraft, she was flown overseas by Crew #8, commanded by George Burton. She was lost to fighter attacks on Mission #69 to Linz on July 25, 1944, with the crew of Robert Warren (MACR #11978).

42-52460 RED RYDER (764th #17)

Flown overseas by George Ryder's crew. She was transferred to the 451st Bomb Group on February 28, 1944, on arrival to Italy. This aircraft returned to the USA in November 1944 for a War Bond Tour.

42-52486 IRISH ANGEL (765th #26)

An original group aircraft, she was flown overseas by Edward peterson's crew. She crashed returning from Mission #66 to Brux on July 21, 1944.

42-52493 (765th #35)

Flown overseas by Walter Grimm and Crew #35 as part of the original cadre. Crash landed on July 15, 1944.

42-52550 (765th #31) FICKLE FINGER

Departed the USA on February 7, 1944, under the command of Glenial Fulks. Transferred to the 449th Bomb Group on arrival. Known as FICKLE FINGER and listed MIA with that group on June 9, 1944.

42-52460 RED RYDER

42-78123 FERTILE MYRTLE

42-78224 #74

42-52723 (766th)
Departed the USA on March 24, 1944, and was assigned to the 484th Bomb Group. Transferred to the 461st. Lost to fighter attacks on Mission #60 to Nimes on July 12, 1944, with the crew of Chester Ray. (MACR #6894)

42-78077 (764th #14) THREE BAD WOLFS
Departed the USA for Italy on February 2, 1944. Crash landed on April 25, 1944.

42-78103 RED RYDER (764th #17)
Departed the USA on April 16, 1944. Replaced the original RED RYDER. Damaged by flak over Ploesti on mission #36, May 31, 1944. The crew of George Ryder tried to make it back by throwing out unneeded equipment and shutting down the #3 engine. Unable to make it to Vis, the crew bailed out about five miles off the coast of that Island. Although 10 parachutes were observed the crew was lost at sea (MACR #5841).

42-78123 FERTILE MYRTLE (764th #19)
Departed the USA for Italy on April 1, 1944. Originally assigned to the 461st, she was transferred to the 484th Bomb Group.

42-78202 FULL BOOST (764th #40)
Departed for service in Italy on April 4, 1944. Lost to fighter attacks on Mission #60 to Nimes, France, on July 12, 1944. Flown that day by Richard Fawcett's crew. Six crewmen were killed in action (MACR #6895).

42-78206 (764th #10)
Departed the USA on April 17, 1944. Assigned to the group to replace SCROUNCH. Later transferred to the 98th Bomb Group, where she was known as DESERT FURY. Lost with that group on August 17, 1944.

42-78202 FULL BOOST

42 78266 #10

42-78212 (764th)

Departed the USA on April 3, 1944. Lost to fighter attacks on Mission #21, May 10, 1944, with the crew of William Wallace (MACR #4657). Leading "B" flight of the second attack section, the Liberator was attacked by enemy fighters and shot down.

42-78224 (767th #74)

Left the USA on April 18, 1944. Assigned to the 461st, then transferred to the 484th Bomb Group.

42-78228 IRON DUKE (765th #31)

Departed the USA on April 17, 1944. Ditched with the crew of James Bennett on April 22, 1944, returning from Mission #28 to Piombino, Italy, on May 22, 1944 (MACR #4917). Last seen about 20 miles off the Italian coast when they signaled they were leaving the formation. No trace was found of the crew after two days of searching.

42-78247 (765th #39)

Departed the USA on April 27, 1944. On October 4, 1944, she was flown by William Waggoner's crew. Lost the #1 engine about 10 minutes from the target. Over the target two more engines were disabled by flak, and mortally wounded the copilot, Norman Schlarp. Unable to stay in the air on one engine, Waggoner told the crew they could bail out if they wanted to. The crew stayed with the aircraft. They landed at the Lansberg-Penzing field at about 1245 hrs. The crew was immediately captured. The aircraft was repaired by German forces and used for experimental flights with the code CL+ZX and German markings. It is believed that the aircraft was destroyed by Allied strafing attacks.

42-78260 (767th)

Departed the USA on April 24, 1944. Lost to flak on Mission #44, June 11, 1944, with the crew of Robert Heald (MACR #5641).

42-78077 THREE BAD WOLFS

42-78436 SHADY LADY

42-78267 MARY E (767th #71)
Departed the USA on May 1, 1944, for service in Italy. Listed MIA after Mission #30 to Wiener-Neustadt, Austria, on May 25, 1944. Lost an engine over the target due to flak. William Diggs and crew failed to return due to damage and other mechanical problems (MACR #5056).

42-78286 (764th)
Departed the USA on May 2, 1944. Crashed due to unknown cause on April 16, 1945.

42-78291 (766th)
Left the USA for Italy on May 1, 1944. Lost to fighter attacks on Mission #60, July 22, 1944, with Fredrick Dunn's crew (MACR #7039).

42-78332 (766th)
Departed for service in Italy on May 27, 1944. Ran out of fuel due to battle damage returning from Mission #90 to Bucharest on August 26, 1944, with the crew of Howard Wilson. (MACR #7962)

42-78417 (764th)
Departed the USA on June 27, 1944. Crashed April 30, 1945.

42-78436 SHADY LADY (766th #52)
Left the USA for Italy on July 10, 1944. Transferred to the 451st Bomb Group on November 24, 1944. Lost with that group on December 18, 1944.

42-78437 (764th #6)
Departed the USA on July 3, 1944. Crashed due to unknown cause on December 16, 1944.

42-78444 ALL AMERICAN (765th #24)
Departed the USA on July 1, 1944, for Italy. The ground crew painted footballs on her to denote the number of missions flown. Her original Crew Chief was Vito Ciprianni. On Mission #69, July 25, 1944, she was attacked by fighters over Linz, Austria. During an aerial gun battle her gunners were credited with 14 German fighter planes destroyed. This incident was written up for "Stars and Stripes." Lost to flak on Mission #108 to Munich on October 4, 1944, with the crew of Robert Chalmers (MACR #8973).

42-78446 URGENT VIRGIN (766th #47)
Departed the USA on June 27, 1944. On arrival in Italy the ferry crew was assigned to the 451st Bomb Group, while URGENT VIRGIN was assigned to the 484th Bomb Group. She was transferred to the 461st. Lost to flak on Mission #108 to Munich on October 4, 1944, with the crew of Walter Chester (MACR #8931).

42-78444 ALL AMERICAN

42-78446 URGENT VIRGIN

42-78497 BUBBLE TROUBLE (766th #6)
Departed the USA on August 4, 1944. Transferred to the 451st Bomb Group on November 21, 1944. Returned to the USA after the war.

42-78499
Departed the USA on July 7, 1944. Crashed on February 16, 1945.

42-78519 (767th)
Departed the USA on July 31, 1944. Damaged by flak on Mission #84 to Ploesti August 17, 1944. The crew of Thomas Moore ditched in the Adriatic trying to return (MACR #8260).

42-78606 BETTY JEAN (765th #27)
Left for service in Italy on August 3, 1944. Transferred to the 451st. Listed MIA on December 26, 1944, with that group.

42-78606 BETTY JEAN

42-78497 BUBBLE TROUBLE

42-78616 SHACK WAGON

42-78616 SHACK WAGON (765th #29)
Left the USA for Italy on August 4, 1944. Returned from Mission #164 on January 20, 1945, with two engines out. The crew was unable to get the nose wheel down because of mud that had frozen at high altitude. The third engine was lost on final approach. The aircraft crash landed, tearing up the nose area of the Liberator. Navigator Seymore Trenner had gone back to the nose area to get his parachute. He died several days later due to injuries he sustained in the crash.

42-78676 (764th #2) OUR HOBBY II
Departed the USA on September 16, 1944, for service in Italy. Transferred to the 460th Bomb Group. Destroyed on March 9, 1945, when her landing gear collapsed.

42-78677 (764th #17)
This Liberator is of great interest. According to the Individual Aircraft Card, this Liberator never left the United States. Photo shows it in 461st Bomb Group markings getting ready for a mission. Because of the #17 on the side of the aircraft we have included her in the 764th.

42-94729 (764th #4)
Departed the USA on March 29, 1944, and was assigned to the 484th. Transferred to the 461st. Crashed on December 24, 1944, on a non-operation flight.

42-78677 #17

42-94732 TAIL DRAGON

42-95287 STRICKLY G.I.

42-94732 TAIL DRAGON (766th #68 / #69)
Departed the USA on March 26, 1944, and assigned to the 484th on arrival, where she was called TAIL DRAGON #68. Transferred to the 461st. Lost to fighter attacks on Mission #69, July 25, 1944, with the crew of Edwin Boyer (MACR #7037).

42-95257 (767th #72)
Departed the USA on May 10, 1944. Lost to fighters on Mission #69, July 25, 1944, with the crew of Holand Olson (MACR #7117).

42-95287 STRICKLY G.I. (766th #5)
Left the USA for Italy on May 10, 1944. Lost to flak on Mission #137 to Vienna on November 19, 1944, with the crew of Arthur Farnham, Jr. (MACR #9937).

42-95304 (766th #78)
Departed the USA on May 10, 1944. Attacked by fighters before the target on Mission #151 to Odertal, Germany, on December 17, 1944. Gunfire damaged an engine, on which the crew could not

feather the propellor. Left the formation after the target. The entire crew of Nicholas Sidovar survived (MACR #10701).

42-95383 LAZY LADY (764th #12)
Left the USA on June 1, 1944. Lost to flak on Mission #69 July 25, 1944, with the crew of Grover Mitchell (MACR 7035).

42-99858 CHEROKEE (766th #57)
Departed the USA on April 7, 1944. Crashed on August 11, 1944, during a test flight. Originally carried OD paint from the factory. This paint was removed after arrival, but the nose art remained on the aircraft.

44-10557 YOU BET ! (765th #27)
Departed the USA on December 19, 1944, and assigned to the 8th AF. Transferred to the MTO. Survived the war, and returned to the USA on June 15, 1945.

42-99858 CHEROKEE

44-10557 YOU BET !

44-40621 IRISH ANGEL/SHE WOLF

44-40621 (765TH) IRISH ANGEL/SHE WOLF
Left for Italy on May 31, 1944. Salvaged due to battle on October 8, 1944. Damage sustained on Mission #111 to Komaron, Hungary.

44-40896 (764th #4)
Departed the USA on June 30, 1944. Transferred to the 484th Bomb Group. Crashed on October 4, 1944.

44-40632 (764th)
Departed the USA on June 6, 1944. Condemned on July 25, 1944.

44-40896 #4

44-41020 JUDY R

44-41039 MALE BOX

44-41016 (765th #35)

Departed the USA on August 9, 1944. Attacked by fighters on Mission #151, December 17, 1944, just before the target. Thomas Deibert was killed by gunfire as he manned the top turret. The aircraft caught fire in the bomb bay and went into a flat spin. Waist gunner Trefry Ross bailed out of the waist window. Copilot Edward Kasold, Navigator, Thomas Qualman, and Bombardier Thomas Noesges were blown clear of the aircraft when it exploded. Thomas West and five of the crew died when the aircraft exploded. The wreckage of the aircraft impacted near the village of Troubkly, Czechoslovakia (MACR #1063).

44-41020 JUDY R (765th #23)

Departed the USA on July 17, 1944. Flown by Robert Chalmers' crew on Mission #151 to Odertal, Germany. Sustained battle damage from flak in the right wing. The hydraulic system was damaged by fighter attacks. Fighter attacks also caused severe damage in the waist and tail and cut fuel lines. The crew was able to fly their stricken Liberator back to Torretta. The crew had to hand crank the landing gear down. On approach they rigged parachutes to the waist gun mounts and used them to slow the aircraft down. JUDY R was declared Class 26, and salvaged on December 17, 1944. She had flown 38 missions.

44-41026 MARY E

44-41091 MISS KAY

44-41039 MALE BOX (764th #1)
Departed the USA on July 17, 1944, for service in Italy. On Mission #108 to Munich on October 4, 1944, she was flown by William Powell's crew. MALE BOX was hit by bombs falling from a higher formation (MACR #8976).

44-41044 (767th #77)
Left the USA on July 20, 1944. Crashed due to unknown causes on January 23, 1945.

44-41046 THE MARY E (764th #71)
Departed the USA on July 17, 1944, for Italy. Ditched at sea during a non-operation flight on December 1, 1944.

44-41069 FORD'S FOLLY (767th)
Crashed due to mechanical problems on Mission #107, September 25, 1944, with Ralph Newtom's crew (MACR #8953).

44-41091 MISS KAY (764th #5)
Departed the USA on July 31, 1944. Named in honor of Col. Glantzberg's (Group Commanding Officer) daughter Kay. Lost to flak on Mission #201-202 to Vienna on March 23, 1945, with the crew of William Baird (MACR #13190). Last observed coming off the target with the #1 prop gone and the engine on fire.

44-41093 (766th)
Departed the USA on July 18, 1944. Lost to flak near Gospic on Mission #117, October 16, 1944, with the crew of Roy Kuhlman (MACR #9192).

44-41113 #22

44-41120 #61

44-41113 (765th #22)
Departed the USA on July 22, 1944. Destroyed by fire on September 11, 1944, during OPERATION COMBAT EXPRESS. During a fuel supply mission to France, the aircraft caught fire when the C-10 "put put" failed. The aircraft was full of fuel drums and burned out of control. The crew escaped. Her pilot, Robert Baker, broke his ankle when he exited from the top hatch and jumped to the ground.

44-41120 (766th #61)
Departed for Italy on July 31, 1944. Transferred to the 484th Bomb Group. Lost at sea on December 9, 1944.

44-41140 (767th #76)
Left the USA for Italy on August 12, 1944. Crashed returning from Mission #132 on November 15, 1944.

44-41158 767th #77)
Departed the USA on August 8, 1944. On Mission #151 to Odertal, Germany, on December 17, 1944, #77 was flying in the #3 position of the lead flight. Attacked by fighters, she had three engines shot out by fighters. The aircraft caught fire and fell from the formation in flames. Max Hailey and six of the crew were killed in action (MACR #10656).

44-41162 STUMPY JOE (765th #38)
Departed the USA on July 21, 1944. Lost on Mission #138 with the crew of Arthur Hughes. STUMPY JOE was hit by flak in the fuel tanks and oxygen system. The aircraft left the formation trying to return alone. Over Yugoslavia the aircraft ran out of fuel, and the crew bailed out. The entire crew were picked up by Partizans. Arthur Hughes and his crew were returned to Allied control on January 18, 1945 (MACR #10490).

44-41158 #71

44-41162 STUMPY JOE

44-41355 (764th #14)
Departed the USA on September 17, 1944. Returned to the USA on June 6, 1944.

44-48757 (767th) MARY E II #71
Departed the USA on September 17, 1944. Failed to return from Mission #161 on January 8, 1945. Thomas Wiley and crew were lost to weather related problems (MACR #10943).

44-48761 (766th)
Departed the USA on November 29, 1944. Lost to flak on Mission #164 to Linz, Austria, January 20, 1945. Joseph O'Neal and five of his crew were killed in action (MACR #11805).

44-48833 (765th)
Departed the USA on October 12, 1944. Returned to the USA on June 8, 1945.

44-48993 GENE'S HARE POWER II (765th #24)
Departed the USA on November 29, 1944. Replaced the original GENE'S HARE POWER. Damaged by flak on February 21, 1945. Dewy McMiller and crew were able to crash land near Russian lines. They were returned to Allied control on March 10, 1945. There is unconfirmed reports that this aircraft was repaired by the Russians and used until the late forties (MACR #12475).

44-49038 BILLIE K

44-48993 GENE'S HARE POWER

44-49375 #32

44-49038 BILLIE K (765th #30)
This radar Mickey Ship departed the USA on October 12, 1944. Returned to the USA after the war on June 12, 1945, by Stan Staples. She flew 32 known missions.

44-49375 (765th #32)
Departed the USA on December 4, 1944. Returned to the USA on June 6, 1945. This B-24 flew 57 missions during her combat service.

44-49390 (767th #79)
Departed the USA on December 4, 1944. Returned to the Zone of Interior on June 12, 1945.

44-49428 (765th #29)
Departed the USA on February 1, 1945. Lost with the crew of Lloyd Heinze on Mission #205, March 26, 1945, due to mechanical problems. (MACR #13197) Last observed leaving the formation with an engine on fire.

44-49428 #29

44-49511 MISS LACE

44-49679 THE UNINVITED GUEST

44-49501 RED HEAD (767th)
Departed the USA on December 19, 1944. She was flown overseas by the crew of William Hettinger. The name RED HEAD was painted by Jack Liendecker, the copilot during a layover at Bangor, Maine. She was named RED HEAD due to the fact that four of the crew had redheaded wives. Damaged by flak on Mission #165 on

January 31, 1945. Ditched in the Adriatic with the crew of Edward Delana's crew when the Liberator ran out of fuel. RED HEAD hit the water about 25 miles off the Yugoslavian coast. As the aircraft sank one of the wings fell over on a life raft, injuring several of the men. Edward Delana and five of his crew were lost at sea (MACR #14228).

44-49511 MISS LACE (764th #15)
Departed the USA on February 7, 1945. Lost on Mission #228 to Linz, Austria, on April 25, 1945. Hit by a burst of flak in the nose area. This burst killed the copilot, William Jones, and wounded the pilot, Lawrence Toothman. The burst also disabled the aircraft, causing Toothman to ring the bail out alarm. Lawrence Toothman's arm was broken. The flight engineer Oscar Scoggins helped Totthman get to the bomb bay, where they both bailed out. The remaining crew bailed out (MACR #14058). She flew 21 known missions. MISS LACE was the last Liberator of the 461st to be lost in combat.

44-49887 BINGO

44-50738 RHODE ISLAND RED II

44-50882 HOT TODDY

44-49623 (767th #78)
Departed the USA on December 5, 1944. Transferred to the 451st Bomb Group on April 15, 1945.

44-49641 (764th)
Departed for Italy on December 5, 1944. Lost on Mission #205 to Strasshof, Austria, on April 26, 1945. Raymond Spehalski's crew was lost due to mechanical problems (MACR #13192).

44-49674 MAGGIE'S BOMERANG (765th #24)
Departed the USA on January 2, 1945, under the command of John Bontempo, who was assigned to the 766th Bomb Squadron on arrival. Returned to the Zone of Interior on June 12, 1945. Replaced HANA POWER, 42-29325.

44-49679 THE UNINVITED GUEST (764th #8)
Departed USA on December 18, 1944. Transferred to the 456th on January 31, 1945.

44-49887 BINGO (764th #6)
Departed for service in Italy on January 19, 1945. Returned to the USA on June 10, 1945.

44-49925 (766th)
Departed the USA on January 19, 1945. Lost to flak on Mission #174 on February 13, 1945, with the crew of Francis Pink. The aircraft crashed near Vienna, Austria (MACR #12489).

44-50386 (767th)
Departed the USA on February 18, 1945. Returned to the USA on June 10, 1945.

44-50410 (764th #8)
Departed the USA on February 14, 1945. Lost on Mission #192 to Graz, Austria. Due to high headwinds the aircraft ran short of fuel and tried to return to Vis. Over Yugoslavia another B-24 collided from below, smashing the bomb bay doors and nose section. All four engines failed, and the crew of Paul Viliesis began bailing out. The navigator and ball turret gunner were trapped and rode the ship in (MACR #12940).

44-50428 (766th)
Departed the USA on February 12, 1945. Returned to the USA after the war on June 8, 1945.

44-50616 (765th #39)
Departed the USA on February 19, 1945. Returned after the war on June 8, 1945.

44-50738 RHODE ISLAND RED II (765th #23)
Departed the USA on March 8, 1945. Replaced JUDY R. Her Crew Chief was R.E. Fox, Jr. Transferred to the 484th Bomb Group.

44-50743 (765th)
Departed the USA on March 7, 1945. Lost to flak on Mission #216 to Bologna, Italy, on April 11, 1945, with the crew of Robert Caran (MACR #13983).

44-50882 HOT TODDY (767TH)
Departed the USA on March 12, 1945. The nose art was painted by Wayne Pifer. Returned to the USA on June 11, 1945.

44-51324 (764th)
Listed as MIA on January 31, 1945 (MACR #11838).

3

484th Bomb Group

History of the 484th Bomb Group

The 484th Bomb Group was activated on paper on September 20, 1943. Assigned to the 2nd Air Force, the Group was officially activated at Harvard Army Air Base, Nebraska, on September 24th.

The original cadre of personnel was assigned to Mountain Home Army Air Base, and was made up of personnel from the 5th Anti-Submarine command then stationed at Wendover, Utah.

The group was placed under the command of Colonel William B. Keese. He and most of the original cadre attended the School of Applied Tactics at Orlando and Pinecastle, Florida. Upon completion of the school they arrived at Harvard, Nebraska, on November 10, 1943.

At Harvard, training began for combat overseas. By December the 484th began their Phase Three training, the last step before deployment for combat operations.

The final inspection before deployment was accomplished on February 14, 1944, and the group received orders to pack up and get ready to move overseas for combat. The first movement occurred on March 2, 1944, when the ground echelon began movement by train for their port of embarkation. The aircraft and crews began their long flight to Italy on March 24th. For the next month the group was strung out across the Atlantic on Liberty Ship and the group's Liberators.

By mid April the group began to arrive at Torretta Field, Italy. They would share this base with the 461st Bomb Group. After several days of hard work setting up camp the 484th was ready for their first trip over the Third Reich.

On April 29, 1944, the 484th flew their first mission to the marshaling yards at Drnis, Yugoslavia. It was deemed a successful mission, as most of the aircraft returned without damage. The group was off to a good start.

Before arriving in Italy the 484th had been designated as a Pathfinder Group. This meant that it would be their responsibility to lead other groups to the target. As such several of the aircraft had radar installed in the area usually occupied by the Sperry Ball turret. By November 1944 the Pathfinder designated was again changed to Bombardment Group Heavy to the relief of most of the flight crews.

The 484th continued combat operations against targets of the Third Reich for the rest of 1944. They bombed targets in Rumania, Austria, Yugoslavia, and Germany. Along with this they flew re-supply missions to Southern France.

January 1945 saw the group suffer through harsh winter conditions at Torretta. Unusually heavy snow made operations near impossible. The group was only able to fly seven missions during the first month of the new year.

On April 26, 1945, the 484th flew their final mission to Spittal, Austria, as part of supplying needed supplies to POW camps.

With the end of the war the group was transferred to the Air Transport Command to aid in the movement of personnel back to the United States. The 484th Bomb Group was deactivated in French Morocco on July 25, 1945.

During combat operations the 484th Bomb Group was awarded two Distinguished Unit Citations. The first was awarded for the mission to Munich, Germany, on June 13, 1944. Despite of heavy opposition and smoke screens that prevented the bombing of their primary target, the group battled their way to the secondary target and bombed the marshaling yards at Innsbruck. Their second DUC was awarded for their mission to Vienna, Austria, on August 21, 1944.

Aircraft and Markings

The original aircraft of the 484th arrived in the standard factory finish of olive drab over neutral gray. The aircraft serial number was painted on the vertical stabilizer as per standard procedure; many of the aircraft were named either by flight crews or the crew chiefs.

After being assigned to the 49th Bomb Wing the group began painting their aircraft in the colors of the wing. Originally the group identification marking was proposed to be a red "hour glass" that indicated time was running out for the Third Reich. A problem arose in the design, however. Since the upper half of the vertical stabilizer was painted red, denoting the 49th Wing, there was not enough room to have the "hour glass" standing upright. It was simply laid over on its side and became a red "bow tie."

As with other groups in the 49th Wing, the 484th painted large numbers on the sides of their Liberators. These were painted on the forward fuselage and behind the waist gunner's windows. These numbers denoted the squadron that the aircraft was assigned. The 824th had the first set of numbers, the 825th the next, and upward through the other two squadrons.

The 484th had an interesting way of denoting the radar Mickey Ships. In most cases these aircraft were assigned triple digit numbers instead of the standard double number. Research has shown that in most cases the number assigned to an aircraft denoted the revetment number to which the aircraft was assigned.

Nose art in the 484th was as popular as it was in all groups. Most of the original aircraft carried nose art. As the war progressed, nose art became secondary. In many cases the aircraft number was placed in the favorite nose art area, and thus the artwork was either omitted or toned down to a simple name.

Liberators of the 484th Bomb Group

41-28765 (827th #310)
This was a radar Mickey Ship. Returned to the USA on June 8, 1945.

41-28780 (824th)
An original group aircraft, she departed the USA on March 2, 1944. Lost to flak on Mission #20 to Wiener Neustadt with the crew of Ralph Hallenbeck, and Squadron Commander William Hendrix (MACR #5666). Just after bombs away the aircraft was hit by flak in the nose, killing bombardier Richard Pearce. Another burst hit the right wing behind the #3 engine in the fuel cell. Fire erupted and trailed back for over 200 feet. Fire also erupted in the bomb bay. The crew bailed out.

41-28803 DRY RUN (826th #61)
Departed the USA on March 24, 1944, as part of the original cadre. Her Crew Chief was Chester Hessler. Failed to return from Mission #100 on October 14, 1944, with the crew of John Robson, Jr. (MACR 9604).

41-28826
An original group aircraft, she departed the USA on February 20, 1944. She crashed during a training flight on March 8, 1944.

41-28803 DRY RUN #61 & 42-94747 NOVETTA MARIA #57

41-28825 PUSS IN BOOTS

41-28835 PUSS IN BOOTS (826th #64)
An original group aircraft, she departed the USA on March 33, 1944. She was flown overseas by Crew #1, under the command of Robert Nichols. Her Crew Chief was Richard Conroy. Returned with major battle damage from Mission #124 to Munich on October 26, 1944. Declared Class 26 and salvaged on October 26, 1944.

41-28836 (826th)
Left the USA on March 24, 1944, as part of the original contingent. Transferred to the 461st Bomb Group, and was condemned with that group on December 18, 1944.

41-28860 T.S. THE CHAPLAIN (826th #501)
This radar Mickey Ship departed the USA on May 20, 1944. Originally assigned to the group, she was transferred to the 451st Bomb Group on October 10, 1944.

41-28890 (824th #200)
This radar Mickey Ship departed the USA on June 1, 1944. Failed to return from Mission #152 on February 1, 1945, with the crew of John Howell. (MACR #11836). The #2 engine was damaged by flak just before bombs away. The flak also cut fuel lines, allowing fuel to escape into the bomb bay. Damage was also done to the controls. Left formation with both #2 and #3 feathered. The entire crew bailed out near Pecs. The crew returned to Allied control on March 20, 1945.

41-28935 ME WORRY (826th #26-Q)
Left the USA on April 29, 1944. Originally assigned to the 461st Bomb Group, she was transferred to the 484th. Returned to the USA on June 28, 1945.

41-28860 T.S.-THE CHAPLIN (foreground)

41-28935 ME WORRY !!?

41-29492 #41

41-28937 (824th #16-G)
Departed the USA on April 14, 1944. Listed MIA after Mission #117 to Munich on November 16, 1944, with the crew of Walter Jehll (MACR #9884).

41-29426 SALLY D II (825th #44)
Left the USA on April 17, 1944. Transferred to the 451st Bomb Group shortly after arrival.

41-29492 (827th/825th #41)
Departed the USA on March 24, 1944, as part of the original cadre. On Mission #22 to Ploesti, May 31, 1944, she took a direct hit from flak. The entire right elevator was blown away. The tail turret plexiglass was blown away, dazing the gunner, Edward Lamb. Damage was also done to the rudder and left elevator. Control cables were also damaged. Paul Schiappacasse managed to control the aircraft by using the autopilot. They were able to fly the ship home. Due to the damage #41 was declared Class 26 and sent to the "bone yard."

41-29502 AWKWARD ANGEL (825th #12)
Departed the USA for service in Italy on March 27, 1944, as an original group aircraft. Later renamed FUEL CELL FANNY. Declared Class 26 on April 17, 1945.

41-29502 AKWARD ANGEL

41-29502 AFTER BEING RENAMED FUEL CELL FANNY

41-29539 TAILENDERS

41-29507 (824th #22)
Departed the USA on March 29, 1944, for service in Italy as an original group aircraft. This aircraft did not have a name; however, there was a picture of a girl sitting on a pillow. She was flown by Keith Rideways' crew on Mission #64 to Blechhammer on August 7, 1944. Returning from the mission, two engines were lost during approach to Torretta. On final approach the other two engines were lost due to fuel starvation. The aircraft crash landed in a field near the base. Two of the crew were killed in the crash.

41-29513 (827th)
Departed the USA on March 27, 1944, as part of the original cadre. Failed to return from Mission #7 to Wiener Neustadt on May 10, 1944, with the crew of Stanley Essman (MACR #4711). This aircraft was one of the first Liberators lost in combat by the group.

41-29519 (824th #24)
An original group aircraft, she departed the USA on March 27, 1944. Transferred to the 461st Bomb Group.

41-29529
Departed the USA on March 27, 1944, as part of the original cadre. She was transferred to the 461st.

41-29530 AMERICAN BEAUTY (827th)
An original group Liberator, she departed the USA on March 18, 1944. Transferred to the 451st Bomb Group and declared MIA on June 23, 1944, with that group.

41-29531 (827th)
This original group aircraft departed the USA on March 19, 1944. Lost to flak on Mission #7, May 10, 1944, with the crew of Samuel Howes, Jr. (MACR #4744).

42-50394 HANGER ANNIE

42-50396 #48

41-29539 TAILENDERS (824th #18-I)
Departed the USA on April 4, 1944. Nose art applied during a stop-over in Brazil. Name derived from the fact that the plane had been delayed in departure, and was close to the "tail end" of the group. Her Crew Chief was Albert Piatek. She was transferred from the group in November 1944. She was credited with 52 sorties.

42-50394 HANGER ANNIE (827th #38)
Departed the USA on May 21, 1944. Salvaged due to battle damage on October 27, 1944.

42-50395 (824th #38)
Left the USA for service in Italy on May 26, 1944. Later transferred to the 455th Bomb Group. Returned to the USA on June 28, 1945.

42-50396 (825th #48)
Departed the USA on May 22, 1944. Her Crew Chief was Maurice Gorst. Crash landed on September 17, 1944.

42-50398 IMAGINATION (825th #48)
Left the USA on May 21, 1944. Salvaged due to battle damage on November 26, 1944, after Mission #124 to Munich.

42-50528 (825th #300)
This radar Mickey Ship left the USA on July 17, 1944. Lost to flak on Mission #169 to Vienna with the crew of Charles Marshall. About 30 seconds after dropping their bombs, the aircraft was hit by three bursts of flak. The #2 and #4 engines were lost. #300 fell several thousand feet before the pilots could regain control. The crew tried to lighten the aircraft by throwing out everything they could. When they believed they were over friendly territory the crew bailed out. (MACR #12455).

42-50569 TIME'S A WASTIN (825th #31)
Transferred from the 8th AF, she arrived on January 7, 1945. Crashed on February 14, 1945.

42-50642 LITTLE MAC (825TH #39)
Left the USA on August 11, 1944. Her Crew Chief was Charles Albone, Jr. Returned to the USA on May 29, 1945.

42-50398 IMAGINATION

42-50642 LITTLE MAC

42-50797 #41

42-50797 (825th #41)

Left the USA on August 3, 1944, after being modified to a radar Mickey Ship. Her Crew Chief was Robert Kopp. On Mission #99 to Vienna on October 13, 1944, this aircraft had a 500 pound bomb that hung up on the shackle. Lt. Cooker and crew tried everything they knew of to dislodge the bomb. On return to Torretta they attempted to land with the bomb still in the bomb bay. On touch down the bomb came loose and exploded, blowing the tail section off. The rest of the plane went down the runway and then flipped end over end. One of the crew was killed, while the rest of the crew sustained severe injuries.

42-50934 LITTLE JOE (824th #28)

Built at the Ford Willow Run plant, she came off the line on June 15, 1944. Test flight were conducted at the St. Paul, MN, modification center, then delivered to Topeka, KS, about July 20, 1944. Departed the USA on August 11, 1944, as a replacement aircraft. Lost to fighter attacks on Mission #137 to Odertal, Germany, on December 17, 1944, with the crew of Charles A, Himmler. (MACR #10679). Rockets fired by fighters struck the aircraft, killing several of the crew. Fire erupted in the waist area. Eight of the crew perished with the aircraft. LITTLE JOE crashed on a small hillside near Wenzeldorf, Czechoslovakia.

42-50934 LITTLE JOE

42-51173 #88

42-51362 #38

42-50970
Departed the USA on August 3, 1944. Transferred to the 461st Bomb Group. Lost to flak on October 4, 1944, with that group.

42-51130 (826th #701)
Left the USA on June 8, 1944, after modification to a radar Mickey Ship. Survived the war, and returned to the USA on May 29, 1945.

42-51147 (827th)
Departed the USA on June 10, 1944. Returned to the USA on July 13, 1945.

42-51173 (827th #88)
Left the USA for Italy on June 1, 1944. Salvaged due to battle damage on March 7, 1945.

42-51362 (825th #38)
This 8th AF Liberator was transferred to the MTO on December 24, 1944. Survived the war, and returned to the USA on May 29, 1945.

42-51694 HOTCHA BABE (824th #24-O)
Left the USA for Italy on August 10, 1944. Her Crew Chief was Chester Coleman. On January 4, 1945, she was flown by the crew commanded by Don Zimmerman. During the rally after the target HOTCHA BABE was hit by flak. Two engines were damaged, and the #3 engine was losing oil. The #3 prop ran away and could not be feathered. The pilot tried to maneuver the aircraft so that the prop would fly away from the aircraft if it broke loose. The prop did break loose, and hit the right side of the ship, cutting a slice as far back as the bomb bay. One blade struck the right rudder as it flew away. Three of the crew bailed out at this point, while the rest of the crew stayed with the ship. The #2 engine had to be shut down. Orders were given to lighten the plane, and the crew threw everything they could out. They tried to jettison the ball turret, but it became wedged in the mounts. After crossing friendly lines the crew managed to find a RAF airfield. Upon landing the landing gear gave way, and HOTCHA BABE made a spectacular crash landing. The crew left the aircraft in a hurry, except for Don Zimmerman. The crew returned to the wreck to find him sitting in his pilot seat with one of the blades from the feathered #2 engine pinning him in the seat. He was able to extricate himself from the seat and join the crew. Except for minor injuries the crew that rode HOTCHA BABE back had seen a miracle. HOTCHA BADE had returned from her 15th mission.

42-51694 HOTCHA BABE

42-51804 #86

42-51851 POT LUCK

42-51753 (824th #21)
Departed the USA for service overseas on August 8, 1944. Transferred to the 376th Bomb Group. Returned to the USA on July 7, 1945.

42-51804 (827th #86-Q)
Left for Italy on August 26, 1944. Returned to the USA on May 30, 1945.

42-51805 (827th)
Departed the USA for Italy on March 31, 1945, returning to the Zone of Interior after the war on May 30, 1945.

42-51806 (827th #80)
Left for service in Italy on August 12, 1944. She was the only group loss on Mission #99 to Vienna on October 13, 1944. She was lost to flak with the crew of James Oakley (MACR #9064).

42-51818 (825th)
Departed the USA on August 23, 1944. Returned to the USA on May 30, 1945. She was returned to the USA by a crew under the command of Robert Boone.

42-51833 (826th #53-D)
Left the USA on September 17, 1944. Returned to the USA on June 5, 1945.

42-51835 (825th #38)
Left the USA on August 21, 1944. Lost to fighter attacks with the crew of Roger Martin on Mission #136 to Odertal, Germany, on December 17, 1944 (MACR #10492). Attacked by a Me-109 from III JG 300 at about 1205 hrs. One of the attacking fighters was damaged, and the pilot bailed out.

42-51851 POT LUCK (825th #40)
Received her name while flying practice missions at Mountain Home, Idaho. The crew was supposed to take photos of practice bomb accuracy. The tail gunner held the camera over the open rear hatch and clicked the shutter. When asked if he got the picture, he said he just hoped for "pot luck." She departed the USA on August 17, 1944. On her 33rd mission she was damaged by flak. Her Crew Chief Stanley Laque worked through the night to get her ready for the next mission. POT LUCK was lost to flak on Mission #169 to Vienna with the crew of Chad Ikered (MACR #12453).

42-51852 (824th #27)
Departed the USA on September 9, 1944. Lost to flak with the crew of William Gaskill on Mission #110 to Augsberg, Germany, on November 4, 1944. (MACR #9678)

42-51853 (824th #201-X)
This radar Mickey Ship left the USA on October 12, 1944. She was salvaged on August 6, 1945.

42-51993 A BROAD ABROAD

42-51882 (826th #51-B)
Departed the USA on August 17, 1944. Her Crew Chief was Robert Tessalone. Lost to flak on February 20, 1945, with the crew of Orgene Colvin, on Mission #168 to Bolzano, Italy. The aircraft crashed near Pontebbo, Italy (MACR #12045).

42-51884 (824th #12)
Left the USA on August 22, 1944. Salvaged on August 6, 1945.

42-51925 EL PAGLIACCIO (824th #14-E)
Left for Italy on August 21, 1944. Later transferred to the 461st Bomb Group.

42-51967 STRANGE CARGO (826th #61)
Departed the USA on September 9, 1944. Transferred to the 461st Bomb Group.

42-51987 (826th #65-P)
Left the USA on September 2, 1944. Salvaged on August 7, 1945.

42-51988 DEMAIO'S DELINQUENTS (824th #15)
Left the USA on December 15, 1944. Salvaged on August 10, 1945.

42-51993 A BROAD ABROAD (827th #700)
Departed the USA on October 12, 1944, as a radar Mickey Ship. It is interesting to note that she left the USA finished as a natural aluminum Liberator. After arriving in Italy she was painted in the dark gray finish common to Mickey Ships. Returned to the USA on May 29, 1945.

42-52002 (824th #16)
Departed the USA on December 5, 1944. Lost to flak with the crew of Ralph Parks on Mission #154/155 to Vienna on February 7, 1945. Flak knocked out the #1 and #2 engines and cut fuel lines. When he believed they were over Russian lines, Ralph Parks ordered the crew to bail out. The crew landed about 35 miles north of Budapest. The crew was returned to Allied control on February 25, 1945 (MACR #12076).

42-52016 #32

42-52016 PATCHES (827th #77)
Left for service in Italy on October 5, 1944. Ditched in the Adriatic returning from Mission #223 with the crew of Aaron Schart on April 23, 1945.

42-52037 (825th #34)
Departed the USA on January 31, 1945. Flown overseas by the crew of Robert Boone. Ditched in the Adriatic on February 5, 1945. Just after bombs away the aircraft was hit by flak in the left wing, damaging the fuel tank near the #2 engine. The crew was able to fly the crippled plane to the Adriatic, where the two engines on the left side died due to fuel starvation. The entire crew survived ditching, and were picked up about three hours later by a rescue boat. This was the aircraft's first mission.

42-52041 (824th #17)
Left for service in Italy on September 17, 1944. Lost to flak with the crew of Eugene Frazier on Mission #169 to Vienna on February 21, 1945 (MACR #12462).

42-52072 THE EUNUCH (827th #72-C)
Left the USA on October 13, 1944. Aborted the mission on February 1, 1945, due to loss of oil pressure on #3 engine. The engine was damaged beyond repair and had to be changed. Returned to the USA on May 30, 1945.

42-52371 FERTILE MYRTLE (824th #23)
An original Liberator of the 461st Bomb Group, she left the USA on February 19, 1944. Later transferred to the 484th. Subsequently transferred from the 484th, date unknown.

42-52438 DAMNED YANKEE (825th #30)
Left the USA on March 23, 1944, as an original group aircraft. On Mission #73 to Szolnok, Hungary, DAMNED YANKEE was hit by bombs falling from a higher formation. Her crew that day was commanded by Thaddeus Walker. (MACR 7687) The aircraft crashed near the target area. Six of the crew were able to bail out and became POWs.

42-52072 #72

42-52490 #59

42-52576 THE RAMP ROOSTER

42-52501 (826th)
Departed the USA on March 27, 1944, as an original group Liberator. Transferred to the 451st Bomb Group, where she was known as LAKANOOKIE. Lost with that group on May 10, 1944.

42-52513 (827th)
This was an original 465th Bomb Group aircraft transferred to the 484th. The aircraft crashed on May 10, 1944.

42-52576 RAMP ROOSTER (824th #15-F)
Departed the USA on March 27, 1944, as part of the original cadre. Involved in a mid-air collision on May 3, 1944, with 42-52660. Forrest Nance's crew was able to regain control and return to Torretta. Salvaged due to battle damage on December 30, 1944. On this mission she was attacked by Me-109s. During the aerial gun battle her gunners were credited with 8 Me-109s destroyed. The crew of Richard Brown was able to return to Torretta and land the badly damaged RAMP ROOSTER. She was credited with 52 known missions.

42-52602 STEW BUM

42-52490 (826th #59)
Departed the USA on March 24, 1944, as an original group aircraft. Her Crew Chief was Maxwell Matthews. This Liberator flew 57 sorties, and was credited with 75 missions. Transferred to the 376th Bomb Group on February 7, 1945. Later transferred to the Air Service Command. Salvaged August 3, 1945.

42-52602 STEW BUM /OLD FLUTTER BUTT (825th #40)
Left for service in Italy on March 26, 1944, as an original aircraft. Flown overseas by Crew #40, commanded by James Langdon. Lost to fighter attacks on June 13, 1944, with the crew of Robert Quilan. The crew bailed out and became POWs (MACR #6416).

THE RAMP ROOSTER in the boneyard.

42-52633 DARLING DARLENE

42-52614 (824th)
Departed the USA on March 29, 1944, as an original aircraft. Transferred to the 451st Bomb Group in June 1944, and was known as LAKANOOKIE II. She was lost to enemy action on July 31, 1944, with the 451st.

42-52632 FLAMING MAMIE (826th #55)
An original group Liberator, she departed the USA on March 24, 1944. Flew the first group Mission on April 29, 1944. She was lost to fighter attacks on Mission #72 to Vienna with the crew of Leonard Poskitt (MACR #7961).

42-52633 DARLING DARLENE (826th #50)
An original group aircraft, she departed the USA on March 20, 1944. Her Crew Chief was James Jones, Jr. On June 9, 1944, she landed at Vis with one engine out due to battle damage over Munich. Later

returned to the group. DARLING DARLENE is one of the few original aircraft from the 484th to survive the war and become a "Home Run" aircraft, returning to the states on May 29, 1945.

42-52635 Ol'45 (825th #45)
An original group Liberator, she departed the USA on March 27, 1944. Failed to return from the mission to Vienna on February 7, 1945, with the crew of Alva Schick (MACR #12179). OL' 45 was hit by flak in the #3 engine and suffered other damage. Unable to maintain formation, she was escorted by Mustangs from the 332nd FG (Tuskegee Airmen). Unable to make it all the way to Italy, the crew bailed out.

42-52641 THE CENTURY LIMITED (824th #25)
Departed the USA on March 30, 1944, as part of the original group overseas movement under the command of Wilson Wilkes. Her Crew Chief was Harold Lynch. One of the few Group Liberators to survive the war. Flew 100 known missions. Salvaged on August 10, 1945.

42-52647 LEADING LADY (824th #27)
An original Liberator of the group, she departed the USA on March 29, 1944. Salvaged due to battle damage after Mission #180 to Linz, Austria, on March 2, 1945.

42-52648 SWEET REVENGE (827th #76-G)
Departed the USA on March 20, 1944, as part of the original cadre. She survived the war and returned to the USA on May 29, 1945.

42-52641 THE CENTURY LIMITED

42-52648 SWEET REVENGE

42-52653 SLEEPLESS NIGHT (825th #26)
Originally assigned to the 8th AF, she was transferred to the MTO on February 10, 1945, and assigned to the 465th Bomb Group. Transferred to the 484th, she failed to return from Mission #226 to Linz, Austria, on April 25, 1945. She was lost to flak with the crew of Patrick Truesdell (MACR #13993). She was one of the last Liberators lost in the group.

42-52658 STUD HOSS

42-52655 FEATHER MERCHANT (824th #17)
Departed the USA on March 27, 1944, as part of the original cadre. She was flown overseas by Robert Bredwell and crew. Attacked by fighters on Mission #31 to Innsbruk, Austria, on June 13, 1944. Robert E. Bredwell and crew were able to fly the crippled Liberator away from the target area. Crossing the Alps, they lost an engine and lost another just after they crossed the coast. Over the Adriatic they lost a third engine. The aircraft broke in three pieces on impact with the water. Six of the crew managed to get into life rafts. They were adrift for the rest of the day and through the night. Just after noon the next day they spotted a ship headed towards them. It turned out to be a German hospital ship. They were taken aboard and given medical attention. They were told they could stay and become POWs, or get back into their rafts. The crew was given 10 cans of meat some bread and some water. They asked the German crew to radio their position to the Allies. Several hours after the ship left six P-38s and a PBY flew over. The PBY returned and dipped his wings. They were picked up and returned to Italy. The PBY pilot told them that the German ship had indeed radioed their position to the Allies. Their almost unbelievable story appeared in " Stars And Stripes" (MACR #3993).

42-52658 STUD HOSS (825TH #35)
Departed the USA on March 27, 1944. Her Crew Chief was Leonard Suiter. This old war HOSS survived the war, and returned to the USA on June 1, 1945. She was credited with 107 sorties and three fighters. It is interesting to note that her olive drab original factory paint was stripped off late in the war.

STUD HOSS after the paint was removed.

42-52660 RUM RUNNER (824th #21)
Left the USA for Italy on March 26, 1944, as part of the original cadre. On May 3, 1944, she was flown by William Abby, Jr's, crew on a practice mission. She collided with 42-52576. About 12 feet of the right wing was sheared off. Three of the crew bailed out after the impact. The rest of the crew managed to regain control and fly RUM RUNNER back to the base. The three crewmen who bailed out were recovered. RUM RUNNER was sent to a repair depot for major repairs. She was transferred to the 454th Bomb Group and crashed on August 22, 1944.

42-52661 SINFUL CYNTHIA (827th #71)
Departed the USA on March 19, 1944, as an original group aircraft. On Mission #31, June 13, 1944, to Innsbruck; she was damaged by flak and fighter attacks. Two engines were shot out during the gun battle with the enemy fighters. Edward Eibs and crew were able to fly the crippled Liberator to Switzerland and land, where they were interned (MACR #6017).

42-52667 TROUBLEMAKER (827th #72-C)
This was an original group aircraft. Left the USA on March 20, 1944. Sustained a direct flak burst in the nose compartment on July 25, 1944. This burst killed the bombardier and damaged the aircraft. She returned to base and was repaired. On October 23, 1944, she suffered battle damage over the target. The crew of Charles Rhine managed to get away from the target and later ditch in the Adriatic.

42-52661 SINFUL CYNTHIA

42-52667 TROUBLEMAKER

42-52668 MALFUNCTION SIRED BY FORD

42-52668 MALFUNCTION SIRED BY FORD
(824th #10-A & #63)
Departed the USA on March 27, 1944. After a long combat history she was salvaged due to battle damage on January 30, 1945.

42-52671 DREAM GIRL (826th #53)
Departed the USA on March 20, 1944, as an original group Liberator. Robert Tessalone was assigned as her Crew Chief. Flew on the group's first mission on April 29, 1944. On Mission #30 to Giurgiu, Romania, June 11, 1944, she was attacked by Me-109s. She was

flown that day by the crew of Clarence Lode. This was DREAM GIRL'S 21st sortie (MACR #6014).

42-52672 OL' 77 (827th #77)
An original group Liberator, she departed the USA on March 20, 1944. On Mission #132 on December 11, 1944, O'77 was flown by Reuben Kaiser's crew. Enroute to the target they had problems with the #1 and #3 engines. The group was unable to bomb the primary target (Vienna) and headed for Graz. Over that target an engine was damaged by flak. The crew headed for the Island of Vis. Over Yugoslavia another engine was lost. The crew was alerted for a crash landing, then told to bail out. Many of the crew bailed out at about 5,000 feet. Several received injuries due to the low altitude. One member of the crew was killed when his chute opened too late. The crew was helped by Partisans, and returned to Italy on December 15, 1944. There is no known MACR for this loss.

42-52675 MISS FIRE (826th #58-I)
An original group Liberator, she departed the USA on March 24, 1944. She flew the first group mission on April 29, 1944. She was salvaged due to battle damage on August 9, 1944, after Mission #65 to Budapest.

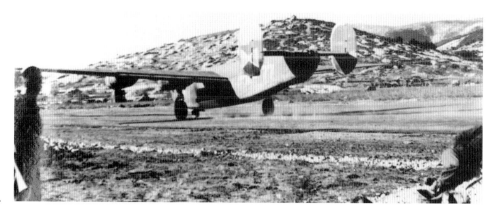

42-52672 OL' 77 landing at Vis.

42-52675 MISS FIRE

42-52683 HOT ROCKS

42-52687 GUARDIAN ANGEL

42-52677 HUSTLING HUSSY (827th #86)

An original group Liberator, she departed the USA on March 20, 1944. She was flown overseas by Donald Haldeman's crew, who was commander of the 827th Squadron. On Mission #20, May 29, 1944, she took three bursts of flak on the right side of the aircraft. Shrapnel killed the copilot and top turret gunner. Major Haldeman was severely wounded. Shortly after leaving the formation they were attacked by fighters. After a running battle HUSTLING HUSSY caught fire, and the surviving crew bailed out (MACR #5785).

42-52678 (825th #47)

An original group aircraft, she departed the USA on March 24, 1944. She was flown overseas by the crew commanded by Charles Crane. This Liberator was condemned for salvage on June 23, 1944.

42-52679 (825th #48)

This original group Liberator departed the USA on March 39, 1944. On June 13, 1944, this aircraft was hit by flak in the #3 engine and had to leave the formation. They were then attacked by fighters. Gunfire caused fire to erupt in the bomb bay, and pilot Robert Willen gave the bail out signal. He managed to bail out from the cockpit side window. Copilot Arthur Roth tried to bail out, but became stuck in the side window and rode the aircraft to the ground. Several of the other crew were able to bail out and became POWs. (MACR #6305).

42-52680 (824th #28)

Departed the USA on March 24, 1944, as part of the original cadre. Crashed on August 24, 1944.

42-52683 HOT ROCKS aka THE UNINVITED (827TH #70-A)

Departed the USA on March 20, 1944, as an original aircraft of the group. She was flown overseas by Wilburn Kitchen and his crew. Her Crew Chief was Arthur Aldene. After a long combat career of at least 70 missions she was salvaged due to battle damage on April 20, 1945.

42-52684 UMBRIAGO (826th #54)

An original group Liberator, she departed for Italy on March 27, 1944. Flew the first group Mission on April 29, 1944. Attacked by Me-109s over Giurgiu, Romania, on June 11, 1944. The fighters attacked from 12 o'clock, apparently killing the copilot. The #3 and #2 engines erupted on fire. The head on attack started fires in the nose and cockpit. The aircraft fell from the formation. After falling about 3,000 feet the left wing fell away. UMBRIAGO was flying her 23rd sortie with the crew of Lawrence Rose. The crew began to bail out before the wing came off. One crewman landed in the Danube River and drowned. Lawrence Rose's foot was severed by gunfire. He managed to bail out. He later died in a Hospital in Romania. Six other crewmen were listed as KIA (MACR #6069).

42-52684 UMBRIAGO

42-52689 SA WRONG GIRL

42-52697 SALVO SALLY II

42-52685 (825th)
An original group aircraft, she departed the USA on March 24, 1944.
Crashed on May 31, 1944.

42-52686 (827th #73)
Departed the USA for Italy on March 20, 1944, as an original group
Liberator. Crash landed on September 14, 1944.

42-52687 GUARDIAN ANGEL (824th #20)
An original group Liberator, she departed for Italy on March 27,
1944. Crashed on a non-combat flight November 11, 1944.

42-52689 SA WRONG GIRL (826th #53)
An original group Liberator, she departed the USA on March 24,
1944. She flew the first group mission on April 29, 1944. She flew
26 consecutive missions without an abort. The nose art was painted
by Arlo Matney. SA WRONG GIRL crash landed on June 12, 1944,
and was destroyed by fire.

42-52690 RUM HOUND (725th #32)
This was an original group aircraft, departing the USA on March
24, 1944. She survived the war, and was salvaged on August 10,
1945.

42-52697 SALVO SALLY (826th #63)
She departed the USA on March 29, 1944, as part of the original
cadre of Liberators. Flew the first group mission on April 29, 1944.
On June 23, 1944, she was damaged by flak. The rudder controls
were cut. Joe Hebert and Willard Pearson spliced the cables together using a bolt and several hose clamps. They were recom-
mended for the Distinguished Flying Cross, but were never awarded
the decoration. She failed to return from Mission #79 to Szolnok,
Hungary, with the crew of Jack L. Abbott on August 28, 1944. This
was the 48th mission for SALVO SALLY (MACR #11702).

42-52700 JENERATOR JOE (827th #75)
An original group Liberator, she departed the USA on March 20,
1944. Her Crew Chief was Richard Moon. She flew 79 missions.
After her combat career she was stripped of guns and served on as
a squadron "hack," and was salvaged on May 4, 1945.

42-52700 JENERATOR JOE

42-52705 TOGGLE ANNE

42-52705 TOGGLE ANNE (826th #52-C & 65)

42-52705 came off the production line at the Ford Willow Run plant in January 1944. She was assigned to the 484th Bomb Group on February 14, 1944. TOGGLE ANNE was an original group Liberator, departing the USA on March 3, 1944, under the command of Vincent O'Shea. Her Crew Chief was Thomas Collins. She arrived

42-527708 BIG DRIP

in Italy on April 14, 1944. She flew the group's first mission on April 29, 1944. On July 16, 1944, she returned with two of her engines out. On 6 August she was hit by flak cutting the fuel lines. Ellsworth Goodall and John Barber managed to get to the fuel lines, and held the lines together using rags and their hands until the aircraft got to a lower altitude and they could repair the line. Both were awarded the Distinguished Flying Cross. It is noted that Ellsworth Goodall did not get his award until 50 years had passed. She flew her 100th mission of April 14, 1945, one year after arriving in Italy. TOGGLE ANNE returned to the USA on May 23, 1945, after flying 107 missions with the group.

42-52708 BIG DRIP (825th #10)
Originally assigned to the 8th AF, this Liberator arrived at the group on January 10, 1945. She returned to the USA on May 30, 1945.

42-52715 VICIOUS VICTORY (826TH/825th #46 & 56)
An original group Liberator, she departed the USA on March 24, 1944. Failed to return from Mission #31 to Innsbruck on June 13, 1944. Attacked by fighters, she was lost with the crew of Syflest Olson. The entire crew managed to bail out and return to Allied control after the war. (MACR #6306).

42-52723 (826th)
Departed for service in Italy on March 24, 1944, as an original group Liberator. Transferred to the 461st Bomb Group.

42-52757 (826th #49)
Departed the USA on March 18, 1944. Crashed June 11, 1944.

42-52773 (825th)
An original group aircraft, she departed the USA on March 22, 1944. Damaged by flak on Mission #22 to Ploesti, Romania, on May 31, 1944. The crew of Jack Crumblias was able to fly the crippled Liberator as far as the Adriatic, where they ditched (MACR #5428).

42-52774 LADY LUCK aka THE PONTIAC SQUAW (827th #84-O)
Departed the USA on March 19, 1944, as part of the original cadre. She was flown overseas by the crew of Alex Bourdo. Returning from Mission #118 to Blechhammer on November 17, 1944, she ditched in the Adriatic with the crew of Henry Mills. During the bomb run she was hit by flak, knocking out two engines. The crew tried to make it to Vis. Before reaching safety the other two engines went out. The aircraft broke behind the wing. Three of the crew managed to escape. The copilot and engineer attempted to swim to an island for help. Henry Mills did not have a mae west, and treaded water for about two hours. He was finally picked up by Partisans in a small boat. They managed to find the remains of one of the gunners. He was taken to Vis and later returned. No trace of any of the other crew were found (MACR #9931).

42-78283 #74

42-52775 THE FLYING DUTCHMAN (826th #00 & 62)
Departed the USA on March 17, 1944, as an original aircraft. Lost to flak on Mission #127 to Maribor, Yugoslavia, on December 6, 1944, with the crew of Robert Somkins (MACR 10222).

42-78114 (826th #65)
Left the USA on May 31, 1944. Crashed on September 10, 1944.

42-78153 (825th #59)
Departed the USA for Italy on March 24, 1944. Transferred to the RAF on October 6, 1944.

42-78200 O MY ACKIN ASS (826th #32)
Departed the USA on April 4, 1944. Transferred to the 455th Bomb Group in July 1944. Crashed September 13, 1944.

42-78224 (826th #56)
Left the USA on April 18, 1944. Originally assigned to the 461st Bomb Group. She failed to return from Mission #164 to Neuberg, Germany, on February 16, 1945, with the crew of George Mason. (MACR #12490) One engine was shot out by flak near Osoppo. Eight parachutes were seen to leave the plane. Three of the crew were taken POW, while the others managed to evade capture.

42-78229 (827th #89)
Left the USA for Italy on April 18, 1944. Originally assigned to the 465th Bomb Group. Transferred to the 484th. Hit by flak over Ploesti on Mission #71 on August 17, 1944. She failed to return with the crew of Philip Wagner (MACR 7682).

42-78268 BUZZ JOB II (825th #41 & 33)
Left the USA on May 15, 1944. Lost to flak on Mission #188 to Wiener-Neustadt on March 14, 1945, with the crew of George Robb (MACR #12946).

42-78283 (827th #74)
Departed the USA on May 10, 1944. Crashed on January 31, 1945.

42-78289 FARGO EXPRESS (827th #44 & #49)
Departed the USA for Italy on May 191, 1944. Her Crew Chief was Virgil Smith. Survived the war and returned to the USA on June 17, 1944.

42-78298 (827th #82)
Left the USA for service in Italy on May 1, 1944. Lost to fighter attacks with the crew of Edward Silvan on Mission #30 to Giurgiu, Romania, on June 11, 1944 (MACR 5821).

42-78304 (827th #78)
Left the USA on May 19, 1945. Survived the war, and was salvaged on July 30, 1945.

42-78327 (825th #49)
Departed the USA on May 15, 1944. Her Crew Chief was Harry Sanders. Survived combat service, and was salvaged on August 3, 1945.

42-78351 THE ROVER BOYS

42-78351 WHAT'S UP DOC ? (825th #34)

Departed the USA on June 12, 1944. Harold Jacobs was assigned as her Crew Chief. Originally named THE ROVER BOYS. Returned on August 22, 1944, with one engine out, a two foot hole in the wing behind the #3 engine, and holes in the fuel tanks. On December 10, 1944, she was flown by the crew commanded by Harold Steinberg. Just after take off the #2 engine caught fire, with flames streaming past the waist. The crew shut it down and called the tower for emergency landing instructions. They were told to dump their bombs in the Adriatic and return. Unable to gain altitude beyond 500 feet, they told the tower they had to land with the bombs on board. The #3 engine caught fire shortly after contacting the tower. The crew were able to get the fire out and restart the #2, which again caught fire. At this point all of the engines quit. The aircraft crash landed in a ploughed field near the base. The crew managed to escape. The bomb load that day included several bombs that had been "booby trapped" to prevent being defuzed. The normal bombs were removed after waiting enough time for the "booby trapped" bombs to explode. Since it was too dangerous to remove the "booby trapped" bombs, WHAT'S UP DOCK was loaded with explosives and blown up. WHAT'S UP DOC had flown 56 missions.

The demise of WHAT'S UP DOC?

42-78351 After name change to WHAT'S UP DOC ?

42-94733 THE FEATHER MERCHANTS #11

42-78364 (826th #51)
Left the USA for service in Italy on June 2, 1944. This Liberator had a very short combat service. She was condemned and salvaged after Mission #36 to Avigon, France, on June 25, 1944.

42-78368 (825th #33)
Departed the USA on May 25, 1944. She survived the war and returned to the USA on July 13, 1945.

42-78371 JOSEPHINE (824TH)
JOSEPHINE left the USA on June 6, 1944. She crash landed on June 27, 1944, on what may have been her first mission.

42-78389 (825th #43)
Departed the USA on July 3, 1944. Attacked by fighters on Mission #62 to Ober Raderach, Germany. The crew of Harry Schultz managed to fly their crippled Liberator to Switzerland, where they were interned. (MACR #7677)

42-78439 (825th #39)
Damaged by enemy fighter attacks on August 3, 1944. The crew of Harry Schultz managed to fly their Liberator to Switzerland. They landed at Dubendorf and were interned. The aircraft returned to Allied control on October 13, 1945, and was flown to Burtonwood, England.

42-78463 (#34)
Departed the USA on July 9, 1944, and was originally assigned to the 451st Bomb Group. Transferred to the 484th on October 16, 1944. Later returned to the 451st. Lost with that group on February 7, 1945.

42-78494 HOT BUT NOT SMOKING (827th #80)
Left for service in Italy on June 30, 1944. Her Crew Chief was Richard Rudkin. Crash landed at Torretta on August 23, 1944, returning from Mission #75 to Markersdorf, Austria.

42-78515 (825th #43)
Departed the Zone of Interior on July 31, 1944, for service in Italy. Her Crew Chief was K.C. Lepley. This Liberator crashed on October 14, 1944, due to unknown causes.

42-78599 (824th #11)
Departed the USA on August 27, 1944. Survived the war and returned to the Zone of Interior on June 14, 1945.

42-78616 SHACK WAGON (824th #29)
Left the USA on August 4, 1944. Transferred to the 461st, this Liberator crashed on January 20, 1945.

42-94729
Departed the USA on March 29, 1944, as part of the original group cadre. Transferred to the 461st.

42-94730 (825th #31)
Departed the USA on March 27, 1944; she was an original group Liberator. Condemned and salvaged on May 4, 1944.

42-94732 TAIL DRAGON (826th #68)
Departed the USA on March 26, 1944, as part of the original group. Later she was transferred to the 461st Bomb Group. Lost to enemy action with that group on July 25, 1944.

42-94733 THE FEATHER MERCHANTS (824th #11)
Departed the USA on March 29, 1944, she was an original Liberator. Her Crew Chief was Walter Rix. Salvaged on August 6, 1945.

42-94734 SLEEPY TIME GAL

42-94737 THE DUCK

42-94734 SLEEPY TIME GAL (ST. LOUIS GAL 826th#57)
42-95277
Departed the USA on March 24, 1944, as an original group aircraft. She failed to return from Mission #22 to Ploesti on May 31, 1944, with the crew of Kenneth Hanson (MACR #5429).

42-94736 (825th #40)
An original group Liberator, she departed the USA on March 23, 1944. She crashed on August 22, 1944, returning from Mission #74 to Vienna, Austria.

42-94737 THE DUCK (827th #83)
An original group aircraft, she departed the USA on March 20, 1944. Her original crew was commanded by Robert Hatch. Made emergency landing due to battle damage on June 11, 1944, returning from Giurgiu, Romania. THE DUCK was salvaged due to battle damage on October 25, 1944.

42-94738 KNOCK OUT (827TH #81-L)
Departed the Zone of Interior as part of the original group. Returned on July 27, 1944, with #2 engine out, and over a third of the right rudder shot away. Survived combat, and returned to the USA on May 30, 1945.

42-94736 #40

42-94738 KNOCKOUT

42-94741 VIVACIOUS LADY

42-94746 VICIOUS VIRGIN

42-94739 (826th #60)
Departed the USA on March 24, 1944, as an original group Liberator. Flew on the group's first mission on April 29, 1944. Declared "war weary," she was salvaged exactly one year after leaving the USA on March 24, 1945.

42-94740 BIG DICK (825th #31)
An original group Liberator, she departed the USA on March 31, 1944. Her Crew Chief was Harold Jacobs. Attacked by fighters on Mission #36 to Vienna. She was lost with the crew of James Porter (MACR #6329).

42-94740 BIG DICK

42-94741 VIVACIOUS LADY (826TH #62)

An original group aircraft, she departed the USA on March 24, 1944, with the crew of Robert Remington. Flew the first group mission on April 39, 1944. On Mission #31 to Innsbruck, Austria, June 13, 1944, she was lost with the crew of Robert Remington. VIVACIOUS LADY was attacked by fighters near Caorle, Italy. Left formation and tried to return alone. Fighters continued their attacks for almost 10 minutes, with VICIOUS LADY being credited with four enemy fighters. Fire erupted in the bomb bay due to fighter attack. Two engines were shot out. The crew began to bail out as the plane lost altitude. Two men were killed when the aircraft crashed into the Adriatic near Marano Lagoon. Four crewmen evaded capture, and three became POWs.

42-94742 (825th #36)

Left the USA on March 29, 1944, as part of the original cadre under the command of Thaddeus Phillips. Returned from mission on April 21, 1944, with flak damage to left wing, left waist area, and tail turret. Survived the war, and was condemned on January 20, 1945.

42-94746 VICIOUS VIRGIN (826th #56)

An original group Liberator, she departed the USA on March 24, 1944. On May 10, 1944, she returned from Mission #7 to Wiener Neustadt with over 212 holes from fighter attacks and flak for her Crew Chief Clyde Jones to repair. She flew 40 known missions. On November 1, 1944, she was hit by flak in the #2 engine. The crew was not able to feather the prop. VICIOUS VIRGIN was unable to maintain formation. After flying towards Italy for about an hour the #1 engine was lost. The crew, commanded by Robert Simkins, tried to lighten the ship to get over the mountains. Finally they managed a crash landing in Yugoslavia (MACR #9701).

42-94747 NOVETTA MARIA aka DOT'S RIGHT/TAILWAIND (826th #57)

An original group Liberator, she departed the USA on March 24, 1944. Her Crew Chief was Joseph Tullier, Jr. Flew the first of her 50 missions on the group's first mission on April 29, 1944. Retired from combat, she became a "hack." Returned to the USA on June 17, 1945.

42-94751 MISS SNOW JOB (827th #85-P)

Departed the USA with the original cadre on March 20, 1944. Crash landed on March 17, 1945.

42-94753 THE PONTIAC SQUAW (825TH)

An original group Liberator, she departed the USA on March 29, 1944. Transferred to the 451st in April or May 1944. She was lost with that group on May 5, 1944.

42-94755 WEARY WILLIE (825th #33)

This ex-8th AF bomber arrived in the MTO on January 7, 1945. She was transferred to the 2641st Bomb Squadron.

42-94747 NOVETTA MARIA

42-94755 WEARY WILLIE

42-94928 #77

42-95275 #82

42-94758 COLLAPSIBLE SUSIE (824th #17)
Originally assigned to the 8th AF, she was transferred to the MTO on December 3, 1944. Later believed transferred to another group.

42-94928 (827th #77)
This ex-8th AF Liberator arrived in the MTO on January 9, 1945. Later returned to the USA on July 4, 1945.

42-95275 (827th #82)
Departed the USA on June 2, 1944. Her Crew Chief was Joseph Baird. Was lost on Mission #147 to Vienna on January 15, 1945, with the crew of Donald Bolagren. #82 was damaged by flak between the IP and the target. The #2 and #3 engines lost power. The bombardier salvoed the bombs as the aircraft took up a heading for Vis. Near Lake Balaton the aircraft was hit by flak again, causing the loss of another engine. At about 15,000 feet the crew was given the bail out signal. The entire crew bailed out (MACR #11287).

42-95277 (824th #1)
Departed the USA on May 12, 1944. Crashed on July 2, 1944.

42-95282 BOOBY TRAP (827th #77)
An ex-8th AF Liberator, she arrived in the MTO on January 8, 1945. Survived the war, and returned to the USA on May 30, 1945.

42-95349 (824th #15)
Left the USA on May 22, 1944. After her combat service she returned to the USA on June 20, 1945.

42-95360 WAR WEARY (827th #87-R)
Left the USA for service on May 19, 1944. Her Crew Chief was Harry Masin. After just over a year of combat she returned to the USA on May 29, 1945.

42-95369 (825th #37)
Departed for Italy on May 23, 1944. Damaged by flak on Mission #76 to Ferrara, Italy. Ditched in the Adriatic with the crew of Henry Dionne. (MACR #7959).

42-95623 JEAN (826th #53)
Departed the USA on July 3, 1944. Returned to the USA on May 24, 1945, after combat service.

42-95282 BOOBY TRAP

42-95360 WAR WEARY

42-95369 #37

42-99851 FLAK STRAINER (825th #14 & #44)
Left for combat service in Italy on April 19, 1944. On Mission #121 to Blechhammer she was damaged by flak, with the crew of Ralph Brautigan (MACR #9974).

44-10484 SWEET GINNY LEE (825th #63-N)
Departed the USA on August 12, 1944. Damaged by flak on Mission #226, April 25, 1945. Her pilot that day—William "Doc" Savage—and crew were able to fly back to Torretta. The pilot briefed the crew to prepare for a tail heavy landing due, to the fact that the nose wheel had been shredded. On landing the right landing gear gave out, and the plane went into a small ditch. The nose and right wing were damaged, along with the bottom of the aircraft. The crew escaped and "ran like hell." Salvaged after the war on July 7, 1945.

44-10550 (827th #73)
Departed the USA on July 17, 1944. Returned to the Zone of Interior on June 25, 1945.

44-40648 COVER GIRL (826th #54-E)
Departed the USA for Italy on June 10, 1944. Her Crew Chief was James McIntyre. Aborted the Mission on November 16, 1944, due to an engine fire. The aircraft crashed near the base.

42-99851 FLAK STRAINER

42-95623 JEAN

44-10484 SWEET GINNY LEE

44-40896 HELLO BUTCH (824th #4)
Departed from the USA on June 30, 1944. Originally assigned to the 461st Bomb Group. Crashed on October 4, 1944, while being flown by the crew under command of John Bontempo.

44-41143 WHAT'S COOKIN'

44-41116 (824th #21)
Departed the USA on August 12, 1944. On Mission #74 to Vienna, August 22, 1944, she was lost to fighter attacks with the crew of John Ruthenberg (MACR #8395). It is believed that this was the Liberator's first mission.

44-41120 (825th #43)
Transferred from the 461st Bomb Group. On Mission #130 to Linz, Austria, on December 9, 1944, she was damaged by flak. The crew of Vern Compton and crew managed to fly the cripple to the Adriatic and ditch (MACR #10248).

44-41136 (825th #33-D)
Left the USA on August 12, 1944. Her Crew Chief was Eldon Dungey. On December 20, 1944, she was badly damaged by flak. The crew of Dave Sheddon managed to make an emergency crash landing on Vis. One of the crew was killed in the landing. Salvaged on December 22, 1944.

44-41139 (825th #30)
Departed the USA on August 11, 1944, for service in Italy. Her Crew Chief was Simpson Nelson. Survived combat, and returned to the USA on June 5, 1945.

44-41143 WHAT'S COOKING (826th #55-F)
Left the Zone of Interior on August 13, 1944. Her Crew Chief was James Yates. Flown overseas by William Dipple's crew. The nose art was applied in the USA. At first she had a reputation as a gas guzzler. Her Crew Chief, James "Tex" Yates, worked on her after arrival, and she lost her reputation. On April 17, 1945, she made an emergency landing at Ancona, Italy. Several days later an attempt was made to fly her back to Torretta. During take off the aircraft did not make it off the steel strip, and ran into the dirt overrun. The nose wheel broke, and the aircraft was left at Ancona. It was salvaged on April 19, 1945.

44-41145 #48

44-41145 (825th #48)
Departed for service in Italy on August 15, 1944. Failed to return from Mission #147 to Vienna with the crew of James Ahearn, Jr., on January 15, 1945 (MACR #111289).

44-41147 (827th #71)
Departed the Zone of Interior for Italy on August 14, 1944. Damaged by flak on Mission #149 to Linz, Austria, on January 20, 1945. The crew of Milton Stansberry was able to fly the crippled Liberator as far as the Adriatic. Two engines went out due to fuel starvation. The crew was able to ditch. They were picked up by a British rescue boat after about three hours paddling in their life rafts (MACR #11535).

44-48765 (826th #33)
Departed the USA on October 8, 1944. Survived combat, and returned to the USA on July 6, 1945.

44-48767 (827th #33)
Arrived at the group on November 27, 1944. Crashed on February 17, 1945.

44-48828 BELLS OF ST. JOE (826th #501-Y)
Modified to be a radar Mickey Ship. She departed the USA on October 12, 1944, for service in Italy. Lost with the crew of Kenneth Larson due to a mid-air collision on Mission #135, February 17, 1945. The other aircraft was 44-49721. The crew was reported KIA (MACR #12701).

44-48988 THE GREAT SPECKLED BIRD (825th #46)
Left the USA on December 23, 1944. Her Crew Chief was Harry Sanders. Returned to the USA on May 30, 1945.

44-49346 (825th #48)
Left the USA on February 1, 1945, returning after the war on June 9, 1945.

44-49371 (824th #19)
Departed the USA on October 23, 1944, and was originally assigned to the 455th Bomb Group. Later transferred to the 484th, she crashed on January 4, 1945.

44-49388 (824th #16)
Departed the USA on February 1, 1945. Survived the war, and returned to the USA.

44-49389
Departed the USA on January 31, 1945. Transferred to the 464th Bomb Group.

44-49395
Departed the USA on February 6, 1945. Assigned to the 455th Bomb Group. Transferred to the 484th, she returned to the USA.

44-49396 (825th #40)
Left the USA on February 1, 1945, for service in Italy. Returned to the USA on May 24, 1945.

44-48988 THE GREAT SPECKLED BIRD

44-49418 PRETTY MICKEY

44-49398
Departed the USA on January 31, 1945. Crashed March 14, 1945.

44-49418 PRETTY MICKEY (827th #75)
Departed the USA on November 24, 1944. Transferred to the 451st Bomb Group on December 21, 1944. Returned to the USA on June 10, 1945.

44-49534 SHE WOLF (824th #26)
Left the USA on February 7, 1945. Returned to the Zone of Interior on May 30, 1945.

44-49580 BONA VENTURA (825th #31)
Left the USA for service in Italy on February 7, 1945. Her Crew Chief was Harold Jacobs. Hit by flak on Mission #193 to Wells, Austria, on March 22, 1945. She failed to return with the crew of Robert Fritts. (MACR #13120)

44-49611 (826th #202)
Departed the USA on December 14, 1944. This was a radar Mickey Ship. Suffered a nose wheel collapse on February 1, 1945, blocking the runway for the rest of the group. This caused a delay for the mission. Returned to the USA on May 31, 1945.

44-49534 SHE WOLF

44-49724 #20

44-49668 (824th #10)
Left the USA on December 5, 1944. Returned to the Zone of Interior on June 24, 1945.

44-49699 THE PONTIAC SQUAW (824th #27)
Departed the USA on December 15, 1944. One of several Liberators named THE PONTIAC SQUAW in the 484th. Returned to the USA on May 30, 1945.

44-49721 (826th #502)
Left the USA on December 14, 1944, after being modified to a radar Mickey Ship. On Mission #169 to Vienna on February 21, 1945, she was involved in a mid-air collision with 44-48828. The crew, commanded by William Dipple, was able to regain control and fly the damaged aircraft back to Vis. On landing the nose wheel collapsed, and the nose was broken off to the bomb bay. William Dipple, and William Hiser were killed. Albert McDaniel died of injuries in the hospital.

44-49724 (824th #20)
Left the USA on December 23, 1944. Returned to the USA on May 29, 1945.

44-49738 IMAGINATION (#62)
Departed the USA on December 31, 1944. Returned to the USA after the war on May 30, 1945.

44-49773 (826th #60)
Left the USA on December 23, 1944, for service in Italy. Returned to the USA on May 30, 1945.

44-49858 (825th #302)
Modified to a radar Mickey Ship. Departed the USA on January 19, 1945. Lost to flak on Mission #169 to Vienna on February 21, 1945, with the crew of Percy Kramer (MACR #12454).

44-49884 (824th #12-G)
Left the USA on January 6, 1945. Returned after the war on June 19, 1945.

44-49890 (826th #56)
Departed for service in Italy on January 26, 1945. Returned to the USA on May 30, 1945.

44-49896 (824th #23)
Departed the USA on January 19, 1945. Returned to the USA after the war on June 9, 1945.

44-49924 (826th #503)
Left the USA on February 19, 1945, after modification to a radar Mickey Ship. Returned to the USA on June 14, 1945.

44-49436 HELLS HANGOVER (827th #76 & #70)
Departed the USA on January 19, 1945. Lost to flak with William Sutton's crew on April 1, 1945 (MACR #12508).

44-49939 ROLL ME OVER (827th #74)
Left the USA for service in Italy on January 19, 1945. Returned to the USA on May 30, 1945.

44-49941 BLACK JACK II (824th #22)
Departed the USA on January 19, 1945, returning to the states on May 24, 1945. On March 16, 1945, she returned from the mission with 57 flak holes in her.

44-49890 #56

44-49957 (824th #200)
Modified to a radar Mickey Ship. Departed the Zone of Interior on January 21, 1945. Returned to the states on May 29, 1945.

44-49988 PAINTED LADY (824th #15)
Departed the USA on January 9, 1945. Assigned to the 459th Bomb Group, and was known as MICKEY FINN. Transferred to the 484th and was renamed PAINTED LADY. Returned to the USA after the war on July 7, 1945.

44-50002 PAGLIACCIO (824th #14)
Left for service in Italy on January 20, 1945. Returned to the USA on June 26, 1945.

44-50239 (826th #502)
Departed the USA on February 20, 1945, after modification to a radar Mickey Ship. Returned to the USA on May 24, 1945.

44-50292 (#89)
Arrived on March 17, 1945. Returned to the USA on June 9, 1945.

44-50319 SNUFFIES'S PUBING MISSION (825th #31)
Left the USA on March 1, 1945. Harold Jacobs was assigned to her as Crew Chief. Returned to the USA after the war on May 30, 1945.

44-50363 (824th #29)
Left for service in Italy on February 12, 1945. Salvaged on June 15, 1945.

44-50364 OUR HOBBY II (826th)
Departed the Zone of Interior on February 12, 1945. Returned to the ZI on June 25, 1945.

44-50378 (#41)
Departed the USA on February 19, 1945.

44-50401 (824th #14 &#400)
Departed the USA on February 12, 1945, as a radar Mickey Ship. Condemned on March 23, 1945.

44-50403 (824th #28)
Departed the USA on January 31, 1945. Believed to have sustained major flak damage on Mission #198, March 26, 1945. She was condemned on March 27, 1945.

44-50406 (827th #703)
Departed the USA on February 19, 1945, after modification to a radar Mickey Ship. Returned to the USA on May 29, 1945.

44-50403 #28

44-50476 PEGGY ANN

44-50437 (825th #44)
Departed the USA on February 13, 1945. Lost to flak with the crew of Richard Helms on Mission #195 to Kagran, Austria, on March 23, 1945 (MACR #13816).

44-50450 MAXIMUM EFFORT
Believed to be transferred from the 454th Bomb Group.

44-50476 PEGGY ANN (827th #83)
Departed the USA on February 18, 1945.

44-50557 MOE'S METEOR (824th #300)
Departed the USA February 18, 1945, after modification to a radar Mickey Ship. Named for Squadron Commander Joel Moe. Survived the war, and returned to the USA on May 29, 1945.

44-50567 (825th #400)
Left for service in Italy on February 20, 1945. This radar Mickey Ship was destroyed by fire on the ground on March 22, 1945.

44-50587 (825th #400)
Left the USA on March 7, 1945, as a radar Mickey Ship. Replaced 44-50567. Returned after the war on May 28, 1945.

44-50557 MOE'S METEOR

44-50567 #400

44-50610 (825th #315)
Departed the USA on March 7, 1945, as a radar Mickey Ship Returned on June 15, 1945.

44-50716 (825th #302)
Left for Italy on March 2, 1945. This was a radar Mickey Ship. Declared excess and salvaged on October 16, 1945.

44-50738 RHODE ISLAND RED II (824th #28)
Departed the USA on March 8, 1945. Assigned to the 461st Bomb Group. Transferred to the 484th. Returned to the USA on May 29, 1945.

44-50739 (824th #11)
Departed the USA on March 12, 1945. Returned to the USA on May 30, 1945.

44-50742 (827th #78)
Left the USA on March 7, 1945. Crash landed and written off on May 1, 1945.

44-50762 (825th #44)
Departed the USA on March 7, 1945. Sustained a direct hit in the waist area during the bomb run on Mission #226 to Linz, Austria, on April 25, 1945. The aircraft broke in two just behind the wing. James Denny and three of his crew were able to bail out. Tail gunner Earl Harrison suffered a broken back in the jump. The survivors were returned to Allied control after the war. This was one of the last Liberators lost to enemy action for the 484th (MACR #13994).

44-50816 (826th #51)
Departed the USA on March 14, 1945. Returned to the USA on May 25, 1945.

44-50821 (826th #61)
Departed for Italy on March 14, 1945. Returned to the USA on May 25, 1945.

44-50825 (827th #79)
Left the USA on March 14, 1945. Returned to the USA on May 29, 1945.

44-50831 (824th #11)
Left the USA for Italy on March 14, 1945. Returned to the Zone of Interior on May 29, 1945.

44-50852 (825th)
Departed the USA on March 12, 1945. Returned to USA on May 30, 1945.

44-50871 (824th)
Departed the USA on April 3, 1945. Returned to the Zone of Interior on May 30, 1945.

44-50919 (824th)
Left for service in Italy on March 24, 1945, she returned to the United States on May 30, 1945.

44-50933 (824th)
Arrived on March 25, 1945. Returned to the USA on May 24, 1945.

49th Bomb Wing Photo Gallery

B-24s return from a mission.

The 451st BG returns to their base at Castelluccia.

THE EXTRA JOKER under attack, August 1944.

THE EXTRA JOKER. Note the large hole in the right wing.

THE EXTRA JOKER on fire and going down.

SLOPPY BUT SAFE over Bolzano, Italy, February 28, 1945.

BURMA BOUND in trouble

THE BAD PENNY over cloud covered Alps.

HARD TO GET and CAVE GAL in the snow at Gioia del Colle, Italy.

42-52072 #72, 484th BG, over the Alps.

Flak damage to #34 (484th).

#38 made it back and ended her flight.

#38 after her last flight.

#72 (484th) and a "little friend."

#72 42-52072 (484th).

#28 from the 451st after a belly landing. Note that not a prop was bent—a tribute to the skill of her pilot that day.

HARD TO GET falls from the formation over Markersdorf, Austria, August 23, 1944.

CANNON FODDER returning from a mission.

44-41113 (461st) burns after catching fire during a supply mission to France.

B-24s of the 451st over the Alps.

Flak damage.

#48 IMAGINATION.

Another fighter kill is added to OLD TAYLOR.

#34 from the 461st BG.

The P-40 used by the 484th BG as a formatting ship.

The 484th's P-40.

The 451st BG rallies for home after hitting Ploesti.

The result of a crash landing.

#40 POT LUCK on the ramp during a supply mission to France.

A little friend escorts a B-24 towards home.

WHAT'S UP DOC after her crash landing.

The 484th BG flies through a flak barrage.

Bibliography

Stapfer, Hans-Heiri, STRANGERS IN A STRANGE LAND, Squadron Signal Publications. Carrollton,Texas. 1988.

Hill, Sedgefield & Michael, THE FIGHTIN 451'ST, Turner Publishing, Paducah, KY, 1990.

Hill, Michael, THE 451ST BOMB GROUP IN WORLD WAR II, A PICTORIAL HISTORY, Schiffer Publishing, Atglen PA, 2001.

Dorr, Robert, B-24 LIBERATOR UNITS OF THE FIFTEENTH AIR FORCE, Osprey Publishing Limited, Great Britain, 2000.